Be God's Guest
Feasts of Leviticus 23

by Warren W. Wiersbe
General Director
Back to the Bible Broadcast

A
BACK TO THE BIBLE
PUBLICATION
LINCOLN, NE. 68501

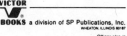

VICTOR

BOOKS a division of SP Publications, Inc.
WHEATON, ILLINOIS 60187

Offices also in
Whitby, Ontario, Canada
Amersham-on-the-Hill, Bucks, England

Cover photo by Bill Myers.
Cover design by Gary Goodding.

70,000 printed to date—1982
(5-0850—70M—42)
ISBN 0-8474-6504-7

Printed in the United States of America

Contents

FIRST MONTH

THE PASSOVER
One day
14th

**FEAST OF
UNLEAVENED BREAD**
Seven days
15th-21st

THE PRESENT AGE

SEVENT

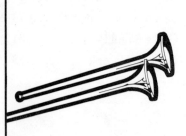

**FEAST OF
TRUMPETS**
One day
1st

**DAY OF
ATONEMENT**
One day
10th

THIRD MONTH

**FEAST OF
FIRST FRUITS**

The day following
the Sabbath
following Passover

50 days

**FEAST OF
PENTECOST**

One day

fourth, fifth and sixth month

MONTH

**FEAST OF
TABERNACLES**

Seven days
15th–21st

Chapter 1

God's Calendar

We are all captives of time. Day by day and hour by hour we look at our watches and our clocks or we consult the calendar. We plan for the future, and we set dates. Many of us carry datebooks to help us remember appointments or special days. All of us are captives of time.

But God is not shackled by time. God is eternal; God lives above time. To God, a thousand years is as one day, and one day is as a thousand years (see II Pet. 3:8). However, God does have a calendar, and it is important that you and I understand God's calendar. When we understand God's calendar, we will know what God is doing in this world, and we will know what is really important in life. Many Christians are wasting time, money and energy on things that are not on God's calendar!

God's calendar was given originally to the Jewish nation, and it is found in Leviticus 23. In that chapter, there is a listing of seven very special events that took place every year in the nation of Israel. These events are called "the seven feasts of Jehovah," and they make up God's calendar.

Importance of the Feasts

We are studying these feasts for several reasons. First of all, our God is a God of order. He does all things "decently and in order" (I Cor. 14:40). God has a plan for His people, and the general scope of God's prophetic program is given to us in Leviticus 23.

Second, we shall study these feasts because they tell us what we have in Jesus Christ. Leviticus 23 does not list a series of funerals or a series of fights—it lists a series of *feasts*. The Christian life is a feast. Being a Christian means enjoying the privilege of complete and joyful fellowship with God. Be God's guest! In Leviticus 23 God invites us to be His guests and to enjoy His fellowship.

Third, we study these feasts because they tell us what we as Christians ought to be doing in this world. There is much to enjoy in the Christian life, but there's also much to accomplish. I trust that, as we study these feasts together, we will learn what it means to participate in the blessing of God made possible through Jesus Christ. We will also learn what God wants us to do.

The Seven Feasts

Leviticus 23 lists seven feasts, and these feasts are centered in the Lord Jesus Christ. As you read this chapter, you will notice the phrase "unto the Lord" repeated many times. The Lord is the center of all this activity. These are not the feasts of man—they are the feasts of the Lord. Sad to say, in John 5:1 we read: "There was a feast of the Jews." You see, when the Lord is left out, then the feast just becomes *man's* feast. It is not God's feast at all.

Passover

The first of the feasts, of course, is Passover. "These are the feasts of the Lord, even holy convocations, which ye shall proclaim in their seasons. In the fourteenth day of the first month at even is the Lord's passover" (Lev. 23:4,5). Passover speaks of the death of our Lord Jesus Christ (I Cor. 5:7,8). Jesus Christ is our Passover Lamb who has been sacrificed for us. Egypt is a picture of the world. Israel in Egypt is a picture of condemned people in bondage to the world. The only way they could be redeemed was by the blood of a lamb.

God began His calendar with the shedding of blood. Unless you know Jesus Christ as your own Lamb, your Saviour, these feasts will have no application to you. You will miss out on the blessing of being God's guest simply because you have never put your faith in Jesus Christ.

Unleavened Bread

Beginning the next day after Passover, and continuing for one week (that would mean the 15th day to the 21st day), they celebrated the Feast of Unleavened Bread. "On the fifteenth day of the same month is the feast of unleavened bread unto the Lord: seven days ye must eat unleavened bread" (Lev. 23:6). The Jewish people not only shed the blood of the lamb and applied the blood to the doorpost, but they also feasted on the lamb (see Ex.

9

12:1-28). The Lord Jesus Christ is not only the Lamb who died for us, but He is also the One who sustains us and strengthens us. The people gathered together around the lamb. It was a fellowship time, a time of removing the leaven (yeast) from their homes. In the Bible, leaven is a picture of evil. The Feast of Unleavened Bread pictures the fact that after you have been saved by the blood of the Lamb, then you should put evil out of your life (see II Cor. 7:1).

Firstfruits

On the day following the Sabbath Day after Passover, they celebrated the Feast of Firstfruits (Lev. 23:9-14). The Sabbath Day, of course, was always the seventh day of the week. This would mean that the Feast of Firstfruits was on the *first day* of the week.

The Feast of Firstfruits is a picture of the resurrection of Jesus Christ (I Cor. 15:23). Jesus Christ is the Firstfruits. The people would go into the field and bring to the priest a sheaf of the grain. This sheaf would be presented to the Lord and dedicated to Him. It declared the fact that the entire harvest belonged to the Lord.

Pentecost

We have the death of Christ in the Passover, the resurrection of Christ in the Feast of Firstfruits and the enjoyment of feeding on Christ in the Feast of Unleavened Bread. All of these took place within just a very short time in the first month of the Jewish

10

year. Then they waited for 50 days for the Feast of Pentecost (Lev. 23:15-22). The word "Pentecost" means "50." Pentecost marks that day in history when the Holy Spirit came down (Acts 2). We have the coming of the Holy Spirit pictured in the Feast of Pentecost. The Lord Jesus Christ went back to heaven and sent the Holy Spirit on the Day of Pentecost. This is pictured at the Feast of Pentecost which was 50 days after Firstfruits.

Trumpets, Atonement and Tabernacles

On the first day of the seventh month the Israelites celebrated the Feast of Trumpets (Lev. 23:23-25). According to Numbers 10, the Jewish people used trumpets to gather the assembly, to declare war, to announce that the camp was moving or to announce a special event. The Feast of Trumpets speaks of our Lord's gathering Israel together, but it also applies to us as New Testament Christians—the Rapture of the Church. You and I are waiting for the sound of the trumpet and the voice of the archangel when the Lord Jesus Christ shall return to receive His own (I Thess. 4:13-18).

Three feasts took place in the seventh month: on the first day, the Feast of Trumpets; on the tenth day, the Day of Atonement; and from the 15th to the 21st days, the Feast of Tabernacles, also called the Feast of Booths. Each of these three feasts in the seventh month applies specifically to Israel. We believe there is a future for the nation of Israel. We do not believe that everything Israel does today is necessarily right. But we do believe that Israel is

God's nation and that God has a great future for Israel. The Feast of Trumpets pictures the gathering of the people of Israel. The Day of Atonement illustrates the cleansing of the people of Israel. The Feast of Tabernacles pictures the kingdom that shall be established when Israel shall enter into her glory.

The people of Israel are a *scattered* people, and they have to be gathered. The Feast of Trumpets teaches this. They are a *sinful* people (like anybody else), and they must be cleansed. This is seen in the Day of Atonement. They are a *suffering* people. What nation has suffered as much as Israel? And yet they shall be comforted. They will enjoy that great Feast of Tabernacles when they enter into their kingdom.

These three feasts in the seventh month have their specific *interpretation* for Israel. But there is an *application* to us as believers. Certainly we are waiting for the sound of the trumpet when we will be called to be with the Lord. We are a sinful people, and we will be examined at the Judgment Seat of Christ. The great Day of Atonement illustrates this. At the Judgment Seat of Christ, everything is going to be made right; the Bride of Christ will be made without spot or wrinkle. We shall then enter into that marvelous time of glory and fellowship with our Lord Jesus Christ, pictured by the Feast of Tabernacles.

These seven great feasts speak to us of the spiritual history of God's people. *Passover*—Jesus died for us. *Firstfruits*—He arose from the dead. *Unleav-*

ened Bread—putting away sin from our lives and feeding on the Lord Jesus. *Pentecost*—the coming of the Holy Spirit. *Trumpets*—God gathering His people. *Atonement*—God cleansing His people. *Tabernacles*—God sharing His blessing in the kingdom with His people.

Between Pentecost and Trumpets (that's where we are living right now) is a time of harvest. During that period, Israel was busy in wheat harvest. You and I are living now between Pentecost and Trumpets, and this means we should be involved in the harvest. Are you involved in the harvest? If you are a Christian, you have come by way of the Lamb and have met Christ as your Saviour. You have experienced resurrection and life through Him. You are putting sin out of your life, and you are feeding on Him daily. You have the Holy Spirit within. But are you involved in the harvest? When the Lord Jesus Christ comes again, He wants to find us faithfully doing the work that He has called us to do. God's calendar not only pictures our privileges in Christ but also our responsibilities.

Be God's guest! These feasts are for you!

Chapter 2

Passover: Christ Died for Our Sins

Thomas Jefferson did many great things during his lifetime, but he wanted only three of them mentioned at his grave for posterity to remember. Number three was the founding of the University of Virginia. Number two was the authorship of the Virginia statute for religious freedom. And number one was the authorship of the Declaration of Independence. He did not even want it mentioned that he was the President of the United States of America!

We know how the Declaration of Independence states this matter of freedom. "We hold these truths to be self-evident, that all men are created equal, that they are endowed by their Creator with certain unalienable Rights, that among these are Life, Liberty and the pursuit of Happiness."

The "Declaration of Independence" for Israel was the Passover. "In the fourteenth day of the first month at even is the Lord's passover" (Lev. 23:5). This was a declaration for them of life, liberty and the pursuit of happiness. It meant *life* because those who were protected by the blood were not slain by the Lord. It meant *liberty* because Israel was delivered from bondage. And it meant the *pursuit of happiness* because deliverance meant they were on their way to the Promised Land.

Lamb Needed

Exodus 11 and 12 gives us a full explanation of the Passover Feast. First, we are told that *the lamb was needed.* The Lord said to Moses, "Yet will I bring one plague more upon Pharaoh, and upon Egypt" (11:1). They had just gone through three days of terrible darkness, darkness that was so thick you could feel it. The lamb was needed because God's people were in bondage. Over and over again in the Book of Exodus the bondage of Israel is mentioned. You must remember that the nation of Israel was a nation of slaves in Egypt. They were not down there on vacation, they were not sight-seeing! They were in bondage. Every unsaved person is in bondage—in bondage to the world, to the flesh and to the Devil (Eph. 2:1-3).

The lamb was needed because there was a darkness over the land and because there was bondage. But even more than that, *death* was coming. "And Moses said, Thus saith the Lord, About midnight will I go out into the midst of Egypt: and all the firstborn in the land of Egypt shall die, from the firstborn of Pharaoh that sitteth upon his throne, even unto the firstborn of the maidservant that is behind the mill; and all the firstborn of beasts. And there shall be a great cry throughout all the land of Egypt" (Ex. 11:4-6).

God has condemned our first birth. The firstborn of Egypt were condemned to die. God rejected several firstborn individuals in Scripture. God rejected Cain and chose Abel. God rejected Ishmael and chose Isaac. God rejected Esau and chose Jacob. God cannot accept your first birth. You may be proud of your first birth. You may say, "I was born into a wonderful family. I was born with a great deal of talent. I was born such a fine person." But God rejects your first birth and affirms that you must have a *second birth*—you must be born again. This new birth is brought about through faith in Jesus Christ.

The lamb was needed because Israel was in bondage. The lamb was needed because death was coming to the land. The only people who could be saved from death were those protected by the blood of the lamb. Just think of it—a little lamb was worth more than all the wealth of Egypt! All of the wisdom of Egypt could not save anyone's life! Only the lamb could do that, and the lamb had to die.

Lamb Chosen

In Exodus 12 the lamb was *chosen*. "And the Lord spake unto Moses and Aaron in the land of Egypt, saying, This month shall be unto you the beginning of months" (vv. 1,2). The Jewish *civil* calendar begins in the autumn of the year, but the Jewish *religious* calendar begins in the spring. Passover meant the beginning of months. When you are born again, it is a new beginning for you. You are born spiritually into a whole new schedule, a whole new

16

program. You enter into God's calendar. "It shall be the first month of the year to you. Speak ye unto all the congregation of Israel, saying, In the tenth day of this month they shall take to them every man a lamb, according to the house of their fathers, a lamb for an house: and if the household be too little for the lamb, let him and his neighbour next unto his house take it according to the number of the souls; every man according to his eating shall make your count for the lamb. Your lamb shall be without blemish, a male of the first year: ye shall take it out from the sheep, or from the goats: and ye shall keep it up until the fourteenth day of the same month" (vv. 2-6).

Please note that it was *God's* Passover, not man's. All of this was wholly of God's grace. God said, "Select a lamb. That lamb must be without blemish; it must be the very best that you have." This speaks to us of our Lord Jesus Christ. In I Peter 1:19, we are told that He is a lamb "without blemish and without spot." They chose the lamb on the tenth day and watched it until the fourteenth day to make sure that it was perfect.

While our Lord Jesus Christ was here on earth, people watched Him. They studied Him, they tested Him, they questioned Him. They even accused Him. When it was all over, they had to admit that the Lamb was perfect. He was approved by God. God said, "This is my beloved Son, in whom I am well pleased" (Matt. 3:17). He was approved by men. Pilate said, "I . . . have found no fault in [him]" (Luke 23:14). Even Judas said, "I have betrayed innocent blood" (Matt. 27:4). The religious leaders had to hire false witnesses to condemn Him because no one could find any fault in the Lamb. Even the demons knew that He was the Son of God.

Jesus Christ is God's perfect Lamb. He knew no sin (II Cor. 5:21). He did no sin (I Pet. 2:22). In Him is no sin (I John 3:5).

Lamb to Be Slain

Exodus 12:6,7 makes it clear that the lamb was not chosen to be admired. The lamb was not chosen to be studied or to be imitated. The lamb was chosen *to be slain.* "And ye shall keep it up until the fourteenth day of the same month: and the whole assembly of the congregation of Israel shall kill it in the evening. And they shall take of the blood, and strike it on the two side posts and on the upper door post of the houses, wherein they shall eat it."

I hear people talking about the life of the Lord Jesus, and we have every reason to appreciate His life, to admire it, to imitate it. But the life of Christ is not what saves lost sinners. Death is coming. Darkness is upon you. You are in spiritual bondage, and the only deliverance there is comes through the blood of the Lamb. It is not the life of the Lamb or the beauty of the Lamb that saves you but the death of the Lamb.

The lamb had to be slain and the blood had to be applied. A Jewish father could know all about this, and his firstborn could still die. Unless the blood was *applied*, the blood could not protect the firstborn from the condemnation that was coming. They took hyssop, dipped the hyssop into the basin where the blood had been caught and sprinkled the blood on the doorposts. Hyssop is a frail little shrub that has no special beauty or strength. Your salvation is not based on the strength of your faith—your salvation is based on the power of the blood. Even a weak, frail little shrub could be used to apply the blood to the door. It is not the strength of your faith that saves you; it is the power of the blood.

God made a promise: "When I see the blood, I will pass over you" (Ex. 12:13). The blood had to be applied to the doorposts of the house, and the people had to be gathered within the house. In the house, the people were eating the lamb, getting ready for their pilgrim journey.

I would like to remind you that it was the blood that purchased their *safety*. However, their *assurance* came from the Word of God. God said, "When I see the blood, I will pass over you." I can just see some little child sitting in the house and saying, "Father, is the blood on the door?" The father says, "Yes, the blood is on the door." The boy says, "Oh, but I don't *feel* safe! I'm the firstborn. I just don't *feel* safe." The father would reply, "Now, Son, you *are* safe whether you feel it or not because the Word of God assures us that you will not be slain."

The blood was for their *safety*, and the Word was for their *assurance*. They could be sure that they were safe because God said so. Some people say, "I've trusted Jesus Christ, but there are times when

I just feel so afraid." Well, my friend, you don't have to feel afraid. Regardless of how you feel, regardless of what your circumstances may be, if you have trusted Christ, you are safe under the blood. The Word of God gives us this assurance. When you believe what the Word of God says, the work of Christ on the cross is applied to your heart and you can have that perfect peace that comes to those who have trusted Jesus Christ.

The Lamb Today

Is the lamb needed today? Yes, because our world is filled with spiritual darkness, spiritual bondage and death. Has the lamb been chosen? Yes, and there is only one Lamb—the Lord Jesus Christ. In Genesis 22:7, Isaac asked, "Where is the lamb?" The answer ultimately came centuries later from John the Baptist: "Behold the Lamb of God, which taketh away the sin of the world" (John 1:29). In Revelation 5:12, the hosts of heaven are singing, "Worthy is the Lamb"! Has the Lamb been slain? Yes, Christ died for our sins according to the Scriptures. He was buried, and He arose again the third day. Now He is in heaven, and He still has on His body the marks of Calvary. He is the Lamb slain for you and for me.

The question is this: Will you make this Lamb *your* Lamb? You will notice a progression of thought in Exodus 12: "Every man a lamb" (v. 3). "If the household be too little for the lamb" (v. 4). "Your lamb" (v. 5). *A* lamb, *the* lamb, *your* lamb.

Can you say of Jesus Christ that He is not simply *a*

Lamb, He is not merely *the* Lamb, but He is *my* Lamb? Have you made His death applicable to your own heart? In other words, have *you* put the blood on the door? Are you trusting Jesus Christ? The Lamb was needed, the Lamb was provided, the Lamb was tested, and the Lamb was slain. The Lamb was victorious!

Calvary is where it all begins. Faith in Christ can mean "the beginning of months" for you. You can be set free to serve God and enjoy life, liberty and the pursuit of happiness in the will of God!

Be God's guest! He offers you life, liberty and the pursuit of spiritual happiness.

Chapter 3

Unleavened Bread: A Meal for Pilgrims

The Feast of Unleavened Bread followed the Passover. On the 14th day of the first month, the Jewish people observed Passover. Then from the 15th day to the 21st, they observed the Feast of Unleavened Bread. This is described for us in Exodus 12: "They shall eat the flesh [the flesh of the lamb] in that night, roast with fire, and unleavened bread; and with bitter herbs they shall eat it. Eat not of it raw, nor sodden [boiled] at all with water, but roast with fire; his head with his legs, and with the purtenance [inward parts] thereof. And ye shall let nothing of it remain until the morning; and that which remaineth of it until the morning ye shall burn with fire. And thus shall ye eat it; with your loins girded, your shoes on your feet, and your staff in your hand; and ye shall eat it in haste: it is the Lord's passover" (vv. 8-11).

During the Feast of Unleavened Bread, the people were very careful not to have any leaven (yeast) in their dwellings. In our next chapter we will think about the cleansing of the leaven from the house, but now we want to focus on the actual feast.

First there is *redemption* (the blood is shed and the blood is applied), and then there is *rejoicing*. First we are saved from bondage and death, and then we are strengthened to live for the Lord. First the judgment is removed, and then we, in obedience to the Lord, remove sin from our lives. Redemption should lead to reformation and renewal.

In I Corinthians 5:7,8, we are taught very clearly that the Feast of the Unleavened Bread pictures the Christian life: "For even Christ our passover is sacrificed for us: therefore let us keep the feast." Because we are Christians we have certain privileges and certain responsibilities from God. To discover these privileges and responsibilities, let's answer four simple questions about the Feast of Unleavened Bread.

Who Could Eat?

First of all, *who could eat of this feast?* The answer is given in Exodus 12:43-51. Moses makes it very clear that no foreigner could participate in the feast (v. 43). In other words, the Egyptians were not allowed to eat of this feast. No matter how wise, how well educated, how rich, no outsiders were permitted to eat of the feast. Only God's people could share in this feast. It was not a matter of morality, it was a matter of birth. If you were born into the nation of Israel, you were then privileged to share in this feast. A servant who was purchased by money could share in the feast provided he had been circumcised; that is, he belonged to the

23

Covenant (see v. 44). "A foreigner and an hired servant shall not eat thereof," says verse 45.

The strangers and the outsiders (the foreigners) were not permitted to eat of the feast. And this is true today! The lamb is a picture, of course, of our Lord Jesus Christ. Those who are outside the family of God, who have never trusted in Jesus Christ, cannot feed on Him. Those who have not been purchased by His blood, those who have not been marked by God—who do not have the Holy Spirit of God in their lives—cannot feed on Christ. They are excluded from the feast.

You may be asking, "What does it mean to 'feed on Christ'? I don't understand that kind of language!" Well, your confession may be evidence that you are an outsider, a stranger, a foreigner. You may not be a fellow citizen in the household of faith. Perhaps you have never been born again into the family of God. Those who were in the house, protected by the blood, were the ones who were privileged to eat of this Feast of Unleavened Bread.

I want to ask you a very personal question: Are you feeding on the Lord Jesus? Some will reply, "Oh, yes, I am. I know what you are talking about. My daily delight is to feed on the Lord Jesus Christ." Others will say, "What in the world are you talking about? How can I feed on Jesus?" Well, if that is your response, then it means either you have never been taught in the Scriptures or you have never really entered into the family. It may mean you are not sheltered by the blood, that you are a stranger, an outsider. If you are not protected by the blood of Christ, you are under judgment.

Who could eat? Only those who were born into the family, or purchased, those who were marked by God and who were protected by the blood.

How Did They Eat?

Now, question number two: *How did they eat?* "And thus shall ye eat it; with your loins girded, your shoes on your feet, and your staff in your hand; and ye shall eat it in haste: it is the Lord's passover" (Ex. 12:11). You see, they ate this feast as pilgrims. They were ready to be called out at any minute. Egypt was not their home. Egypt was a place of bondage, a place where they were under the sentence of condemnation. Israel was destined for the Promised Land. That was their real home. They ate this feast as pilgrims who were ready to be called out at God's command. You and I must live the Christian life as those who may be called out at any minute.

For one thing, we don't know when we might die. Even more than that, we don't know when Jesus may return. We don't know the day or the hour. We want to be faithfully doing our task when the Lord returns. As Israel fed on the lamb, they were feeding as pilgrims who were ready for relocation. They also ate in haste. My mother always told me not to gulp down my food. We taught our children to eat their food leisurely and not to be in haste. But not so with this feast! These pilgrims ate in haste so they would

25

not be caught lingering behind when the summons came to move out.

Some Christians today are living as though there is no crisis. I'm not saying we should become nervous and upset. Nor am I suggesting we should be running around like the proverbial chicken with her head cut off. But the suggestion is made here that, just like Israel in Egypt, we are living in crisis times. A crisis was at hand in the land of Egypt, and the Jews were to eat in haste lest they be caught unprepared. Lot lingered, and the angels had to drag him out of Sodom. Then his wife turned back and looked in disobedience, and she was judged (see Gen. 19:15-26).

Are you eating in haste? I mean by that, are you keeping alert to the fact that Jesus may come? "Wherefore gird up the loins of your mind, be sober, and hope to the end for the grace that is to be brought unto you at the revelation of Jesus Christ" (I Pet. 1:13). They had their loins girded. We must have our minds girded for action. We must not allow our minds to get filled with all sorts of extraneous things. We should have the loins of our mind girded up. Pull your mind together, pull your thoughts together! Shoes on your feet, your staff in your hand, waiting to be called!

How did they eat? They ate as a family. The entire household was involved in this feast. If the household was too little for the lamb, then the neighbors came along and two households were joined. It was a family feast. All of the people of God, under the blood, fed on the lamb. It is a picture of God's people today, united as one family.

They ate the feast at night. You and I are living in a time of darkness. This world is dark. The light of God's Word is shining in this dark world, and it is the only trustworthy light that we have. We are living in a time of darkness and crisis, and we are feeding on Jesus Christ.

What Did They Eat?

Who could eat? Those who belonged to the family, those under the blood. How did they eat? As pilgrims in haste, as a family, waiting to be called. Now a third question: *What did they eat?* For one thing, they ate the lamb. They were not *saved* by eating the lamb. They were saved by applying the blood. Some Christians do not take time daily to feed on Jesus Christ, and they are missing a lot. They say, "Oh, yes, I'm saved by the blood, but I don't spend much time reading my Bible. I don't spend much time praying. I'm not feeding on the Lord Jesus." No wonder they lack strength for their pilgrim journey!

This lamb, you will notice, was roasted with fire. This speaks of the judgment of Calvary. They did not eat the lamb raw. People talk about the life of Jesus, the example of Jesus, the teaching of Jesus, but they don't mention the death of Jesus. They don't want the cross. But that is trying to eat Jesus Christ raw. (These, of course, are symbolic terms, but the lesson is very clear.) The lamb had to go

27

through the fire, and Jesus Christ had to go through the fire of judgment for us.

I notice that they were supposed to eat *all* of the lamb. Anything that was left over was to be burned in fire. We need *all* of Jesus Christ, a whole Christ, and not just a part of Jesus. We need the whole Saviour. The Lord Jesus went through the fires of Calvary for us. His blood was shed for us, and we need to feed on *all* of the Lord Jesus—the warnings and the promises, the principles and the admonitions. We need *all* of the Lord Jesus—His perfect life, His death, His resurrection, His ascension. We need all of Him, and as we feed on Him, we are obeying the Lord.

Exodus 12:4 makes it clear that everybody had his own particular capacity: "Every man according to his eating shall make your count for the lamb." Not every Christian has the same appetite. Some saints of God are so filled up with worldly things, they've lost their appetite for the Lord Jesus. But some believers so love the Lord Jesus that they feed on Him moment by moment.

They also ate the bitter herbs. This reminded them of their suffering in Egypt. In the Book of Deuteronomy, Moses over and over again says, "Now, you remember you were in bondage in the land of Egypt. Remember that God delivered you from that bondage." Alas, too often the Jews forgot. We are not supposed to remember our past sins— they have been taken care of and God has forgotten them—but don't ever forget what your life was like before you met the Lord Jesus. The next time you

28

think God has been hard on you and the Christian life is too difficult, just remember that you once were in bondage to sin and the Lord Jesus delivered you. They ate the bitter herbs to remind them they had suffered under bondage.

They also ate the unleavened bread. Leaven (yeast) is a picture of sin. There was not supposed to be any yeast in their homes for that whole week. They had to cleanse their homes and their lives of any leaven.

Now, please note that they were not saved by eating the lamb—they were saved by trusting God and applying the blood. They were not saved by putting away the leaven—they put away the leaven because they were saved. It is not by cleaning up your life that you are rescued from condemnation— it is by trusting the blood of the Lord Jesus Christ.

Why Did They Eat?

One final question: *Why did they eat?* They did not eat the lamb to be saved because they were saved by the blood. They ate the lamb because they needed the strength and the nourishment for their pilgrim journey. You and I are pilgrims on the way to glory (I Pet. 2:11). We need to feed on Jesus Christ through the Word or we will faint on the way. As we feed on Him, we are strengthened for our pilgrim journey.

Are you feeding on Jesus Christ, or are you one of the outsiders? Are you feeding on Him as a pilgrim ready to be called away? Are you enjoying *all* of the Lord Jesus? Have you put sin out of your life? Are you being strengthened day by day as you feed on Him? This is the meaning of the Feast of Unleavened Bread. Let us keep this feast to the glory of God as we feed on the Lord Jesus and wait expectantly for His call.

Be God's guest! You need strength for the journey!

Chapter 4

Unleavened Bread: Put Away Sin!

The Christian life is a feast. It is not a famine or a fast or a funeral. The Christian life is a feast, and Leviticus 23 outlines for us the seven feasts of Jehovah that picture what God does for His people. These feasts present to us what Jesus Christ has done for us and what He will do in the future. The series of feasts begins with Passover. If you are going to be God's guest at His feast, you have to come by way of the blood, the blood of the Lamb, the Lord Jesus Christ.

The second feast is the Feast of Unleavened Bread. Passover was on the 14th day of the first month, and from the 15th day to the 21st day they celebrated the Feast of Unleavened Bread. We read in Exodus 12:15: "Seven days shall ye eat unleavened bread; even the first day ye shall put away leaven out of your houses: for whosoever eateth leavened bread from the first day until the seventh day, that soul shall be cut off from Israel." And in verses 19 and 20 we read: "Seven days shall there be no leaven found in your houses: for whosoever eateth that which is leavened, even that soul shall be

31

cut off from the congregation of Israel, whether he be a stranger, or born in the land. Ye shall eat nothing leavened; in all your habitations shall ye eat unleavened bread." Note also Exodus 13:7: "Unleavened bread shall be eaten seven days; and there shall no leavened bread be seen with thee, neither shall there be leaven seen with thee in all thy quarters." God made it very clear that during these seven days they were to get rid of all the leaven.

Leaven, as you know, is yeast. Yeast is that wonderful substance that makes bread dough rise. In the Bible leaven is a symbol of sin. Why would God use leaven as a picture of sin? To begin with, leaven is a small thing, but it spreads secretly and quietly, just like sin. Really, it infects the dough. You don't hear the dough rising—you see it rise. Leaven is small but powerful, and it can spread quickly. When it spreads, it always puffs up. Isn't that a perfect picture of sin? We read in I Corinthians 5:1,2: "It is reported commonly that there is fornication among you, . . . and ye are puffed up." There was sin—leaven—in the church at Corinth, and the fellowship was infected.

Leaven is a picture of sin. Sin gets into our lives very quietly, very secretly, and it starts to spread if we do not put it out of our lives. It will grow, it will puff up. So often when sin takes hold in a person's life, that person gets proud, haughty, sometimes even proud of the fact that he is living such a "free life."

Please note that the people were not saved from Egypt by getting rid of the leaven. They got rid of the leaven because they had been delivered from Egypt. You aren't saved because you have put sin out of your life. You go to heaven because you have trusted Christ as your Saviour. You are safe under the blood of the Lamb.

But let those who "nameth the name of Christ depart from iniquity" (II Tim. 2:19). There is a very definite responsibility on the part of the believer to put sin away from his life. We should "cleanse ourselves from all filthiness of the flesh and spirit, perfecting holiness in the fear of God" (II Cor. 7:1).

In the Bible there are six different kinds of leaven mentioned—different sins that we must put out of our lives. You may be wondering, "Why is my Christian life faltering? Why am I at a standstill? Why am I going backward?" Or you may be saying, "I wonder why our church is not growing as it should? Or why don't we have a living and vital fellowship?" Maybe there is leaven that has to be dealt with.

The Old Leaven

To begin with, we must get rid of *the old leaven.* "Purge out therefore the old leaven, that ye may be a new lump, as ye are unleavened. For even Christ our passover is sacrificed for us" (I Cor. 5:7). I think Paul was referring to that which belongs to the old life. Don't drag into your new life the leaven from the old life. Abraham did that, you know. Twice he told his wife, "Now, we are going to lie. You must tell everyone that you are my sister. If you tell them you are my wife, they might kill me to get you." (She

33

must have been a very beautiful woman for Abraham to have that kind of a fear!) Abraham dragged into his new life some leaven from the old life, and of course, it got him into trouble.

I think in I Corinthians 5 Paul was also suggesting that the man in the church who was living in sin was a part of the old leaven. Paul told the church to discipline the offender. "Ye are puffed up, and have not rather mourned, that he that hath done this deed might be taken away from among you. . . . Your glorying is not good. Know ye not that a little leaven leaveneth the whole lump?" (vv. 2,6).

If our churches do not deal with sin, the sin will grow and will infect other people. Before long you will have a real problem on your hands. Church discipline is not a policeman's finding a culprit and throwing him in jail. Church discipline is a broken-hearted shepherd's finding a wayward sheep, weeping, praying and trying to restore him.

The Leaven of Malice and Wickedness

First Corinthians 5:8 states, "Not with old leaven, neither with the leaven of malice and wickedness; but with the unleavened bread of sincerity and truth."* *Malice and wickedness* are like leaven. Malice is carrying bad feelings in your heart against somebody. Whenever you hear that your enemy

---

*The phrase "keep the feast" does not imply that Christians today are obligated to keep the Old Testament feasts. "Keep the feast" means, "Let us live our Christian life as a feast." (See Col. 2:13-16; Gal. 4:1-11.)

has had success, it makes you envious. Whenever you hear he has had trouble, it makes you happy. Malice is that grievous poison down inside that keeps Christians from getting along with each other. Like leaven, it will grow and infect whole families and churches.

The Bible admonishes us to lay aside "all malice, and all guile, and hypocrisies, and envies, and all evil speakings" (I Pet. 2:1). These sins can spread in a church or in a family. Some families are torn apart because of malice and hard feelings. We would have revival in our churches if people would just apologize to each other and put the old leaven of malice and wickedness out of their lives.

The Leaven of Hypocrisy

A third kind of leaven is given in Luke 12:1—*the leaven of hypocrisy.* "Beware ye of the leaven of the Pharisees," said Jesus, "which is hypocrisy."

Hypocrisy means deliberately pretending. None of us lives up to his ideals; none of us is all that he would like to be or all that he could be in Christ. But that is not hypocrisy. Falling short of our ideals is not hypocrisy. Pretending we have reached our ideals when we have not—that is hypocrisy. I suppose the clearest diagnosis of hypocrisy anywhere in the Bible is in Matthew 23 where our Lord Jesus took the scribes and Pharisees and held them up to God's X ray. "Woe unto you, scribes and Pharisees, hypocrites! for ye are like unto whited sepulchres, which indeed appear beautiful outward, but are within full of dead men's bones, and of all uncleanness" (v. 27). Hypocrisy is pretense, and like leaven, it grows. First we pretend about our prayer life, then we start pretending about our giving, and then we start pretending about our witnessing. Before long we really believe all of this pretense! The leaven has grown in our lives, and our hypocrisy increases.

Hypocrisy is a terrible sin because it keeps us from sincerity and truth. You cannot live the Christian life successfully apart from truth. So let's be aware of the old leaven—anything from the old life. Let's get rid of those old habits, those old associations, that are infecting our lives. Let's put away the leaven of malice and wickedness and the leaven of hypocrisy.

The Leaven of Herod

In Mark 8:15 the Lord Jesus warned His disciples about *the leaven of Herod.* Herod, of course, was the ruler of part of the land of Palestine, and he was a compromiser. Herod's philosophy was to go along with the Jews to get what he wanted and to cooperate with the Romans to get what he wanted. He was a compromiser. The leaven of Herod is the leaven of worldliness and compromise.

I hear people saying that the church has to get into the world and do what the world does in order to win the world. That philosophy is exactly opposite to the biblical pattern. The Bible teaches us that the church has to be unlike the world to be able to attract the world. We don't have to become sick in order to help sick people. We don't have to become ignorant to help ignorant people. The church has to maintain a separated, unworldly attitude if we are going to win people to Christ. Beware of the leaven of worldliness and compromise.

The Leaven of the Sadducees

In Matthew 16:6 our Lord warns about *the leaven of the Sadducees,* which is unbelief. The Sadducees were the "modernists" of their day. They didn't believe in angels, spirits or the resurrection from the dead (see Acts 23:8).

Believe the Word of God. Believe what God has to say, accept it and act upon it. If someone comes along and says, "We have to rethink the Bible," be careful. I don't think the Bible was given for me to judge. It was given to judge me. I am the one who needs to be judged by the Word of God, and I don't have the right to judge it. Study it—yes. Read it—of course. Meditate on it—absolutely. But question it—absolutely not! Beware of the leaven of the Sadducees, which is unbelief.

Young people going off to colleges and universities are told that they can't trust the Bible, that it's an outdated, ancient book, a record of man's search for God. If you start believing that sort of misinformation, you will end up in trouble. The leaven of unbelief will grow, and before you know it, you will lose the power of the Word of God in your life. Then how will you stand? What will be the foundation for your life?

The Leaven of False Doctrine

Finally, in Galatians 5:9 there is a warning about a sixth kind of leaven—*false doctrine.* The Galatian churches had been invaded by the Judaizers, the legalists, who said, "You are saved by faith in Jesus Christ *plus* keeping the Law. You are sanctified by faith in Christ *plus* being obedient to the Law."

We have legalists today—people who give us rules and regulations that are supposed to make us spiritual. "A little leaven leaveneth the whole lump," Paul warned (Gal. 5:9). What leaven was he talking about? "This persuasion [false doctrine] cometh not of him that calleth you" (v. 8). A little bit of false doctrine gets into the church, and before you know it, it spreads and you have a church turning from the truth. You may say, "Well, it's not important for us to believe these doctrines." Yes, it is! It is very important, because if false doctrine gets in, it will infect the body of believers, it will create problems, it will rob the church of power. It will grieve the Holy Spirit, and the church will lose its witness for the Lord.

God says, "Put away the leaven." Don't let it even be *seen* in your lives! Get rid of the old leaven from the old life; put away malice and wickedness, hypocrisy, worldliness and compromise, unbelief and false doctrine. "Search me, O God, and know my heart . . . see if there be any wicked way in me" (Ps. 139:23,24).

Be God's guest! He offers you purity of life!

Chapter 5

Firstfruits: Harvest Celebration

The Feast of the Firstfruits took place the day after the Sabbath following Passover. Passover would come on the 14th day of the first month, then the Feast of Unleavened Bread from the 15th day to the 21st day. The day following the Sabbath Day, after Passover, was the Feast of Firstfruits, described for us in Leviticus 23:10-14.

"Speak unto the children of Israel, and say unto them, When ye be come into the land which I give unto you, and shall reap the harvest thereof, then ye shall bring a sheaf of the firstfruits of your harvest unto the priest: and he shall wave the sheaf before the Lord, to be accepted for you: on the morrow after the sabbath the priest shall wave it. And ye shall offer that day when ye wave the sheaf an he lamb without blemish of the first year for a burnt-offering unto the Lord. And the meat-offering thereof shall be two tenth deals of fine flour mingled with oil, an offering made by fire unto the Lord for a sweet savour: and the drink-offering thereof shall be of wine, the fourth part of an hin. And ye shall eat neither bread, nor parched corn, nor green ears, until the selfsame day that ye have brought an offering unto your God: it shall be a statute for ever throughout your generations in all your dwellings."

Give God Your Best

"Firstfruits," of course, applied to harvesttime. During that first month, it would have been the beginning of the barley and the flax harvest.

In the Feast of the Firstfruits God is saying to us, "Bring Me the best. Bring Me the first of everything. I must get first place in your life." Before the people were allowed to eat of the harvest or make any bread, they had to bring the first sheaf to the Lord and wave it before Him in dedication. The burnt-offering (Lev. 23:12) speaks of dedication, giving our all to God. In New Testament terms, this is Romans 12:1: "Present your bodies a living sacrifice, holy, acceptable unto God."

The sheaves were brought to the Lord as an acknowledgment of His goodness. There would not even be a harvest were it not for the goodness of God! Israel would not even be in their land were it not for the faithfulness of the Lord. The Feast of the Firstfruits was a reminder to them that everything they had came from God.

Surely, *all* of us ought to be praising the Lord, for were it not for His goodness, we would have nothing. Some may have more than others, but whatever we have has come from God. "Trust in the Lord with all thine heart; and lean not unto thine own understanding. In all thy ways acknowledge him, and he shall direct thy paths. Be not wise in thine own eyes: fear the Lord, and depart from evil. It shall be health to thy navel, and marrow to thy bones. Honour the Lord with thy substance, and with the firstfruits of all thine increase: so shall thy barns be filled with plenty, and thy presses shall burst out with new wine" (Prov. 3:5-10). God gave the promise to His Old Testament people that if they were faithful in their giving, putting God first, He would abundantly bless them.

But let me make it clear that the New Testament Church has not been promised earthly riches. God has promised to meet our needs (Phil. 4:19), but He has not promised riches in return for obedience. We are not promised that our barns will be filled to running over. Some of God's choicest people in this world are poor. Jesus was poor. The Apostle Paul wrote: "As poor, yet making many rich" (II Cor. 6:10). There is no special guarantee that if you give God first place in your life, you will become a million-aire. But there is a guarantee that He will always take care of you.

"Seek ye first the kingdom of God, and his righteousness; and all these things shall be added unto you" (Matt. 6:33). Put Him first, and He will care for you. When you put the Lord Jesus Christ first in your life, then God *has* to take care of you. I am not saying that God will make you the wealthiest person in town. What I am saying is that you will never lack for any good thing. He will always care for us and give us far more than we deserve.

The Feast of Firstfruits says to us, "Put God first in

41

your life! Give Him the firstfruits, and give Him the *best* of the firstfruits."

The sheaf was presented to God along with some other offerings. The meal-offering of fine flour speaks, of course, of the character of our Lord Jesus Christ. The burnt-offering in Leviticus 23:12 speaks of the total surrender of our Lord Jesus Christ. The oil reminds us of the Holy Spirit. The wine reminds us of joy. We bring the offering of our firstfruits to God *through the Lord Jesus Christ.* We do not bring our firstfruits to the Lord in *our* name or because of *our* holiness. We bring everything through Christ (I Pet. 2:5). It is because of *His* sacrifice and *His* perfection that we have the privilege of bringing our best to God. And we do it joyfully. In the Old Testament, wine is a picture of joy. We don't bring our offering to the Lord grudgingly because the Lord loves a cheerful giver (see II Cor. 9:7).

Are you giving Him the firstfruits? Or do you give Him the leftovers? How many people there are who burn the candle of their lives and then blow the smoke in God's face. How many there are who use their money, time, energy and resources for their own selfish pleasure, and then if there's something left over, they give it to the Lord. This is not what Firstfruits is saying to us. This feast declares, "God gets the first. He gets the best. Put Him first, and He will bless you."

The Resurrection of Christ

The Feast of Firstfruits also speaks to us of the

resurrection of Jesus Christ from the dead. "But now is Christ risen from the dead, and become the firstfruits of them that slept. For since by man came death, by man came also the resurrection of the dead. For as in Adam all die, even so in Christ shall all be made alive. But every man in his own order: Christ the firstfruits; afterward they that are Christ's at his coming. Then cometh the end, when he shall have delivered up the kingdom to God, even the Father" (I Cor. 15:20-24). When our Lord Jesus Christ arose from the dead, He became the first-fruits. He was that grain of wheat that was planted in the ground (John 12:24), and He is the One who is going to bring the harvest.

Please note that the Feast of Firstfruits took place the day after the Sabbath following Passover. The Sabbath Day is always the seventh day. This means Firstfruits took place on *the first day of the week!* Our Lord Jesus Christ arose from the dead on the first day of the week. Today we do not worship on the Sabbath Day; rather, we gather to worship on the first day of the week as the New Testament church did (see Acts 20:7; I Cor. 16:1,2).

Our Lord Jesus Christ arose from the dead and became "the firstfruits." But what does this mean? It means that God has accepted Christ as a guarantee of the whole harvest. All believers will one day be raised from the dead! How do we know? *Because Jesus is the firstfruits of them that sleep!* When a believer dies, it is only sleep—the body goes to sleep, but the soul goes home to be with the Lord. One day there shall be a resurrection, a harvest. In

43

my pastoral ministry, I have gone out to the cemetery with grieving people to lay a body to rest. Sometimes there has been just a little grave into which we placed the body of a baby or a little child. Sometimes it has been an aged saint who has lived a long and fruitful life. The cemetery is a field of seeds. It is "God's acre." One of these days there will be a resurrection, a harvest. Those bodies that were planted in the ground like a seed, in weakness, will be raised in power. Bodies sown in corruption will be raised in incorruption. Bodies sown in humiliation will be raised in glory (see 15:42-44). The cemetery will be a harvest place one of these days because Jesus Christ is the firstfruits. "Because I live, ye shall live also" (John 14:19).

Because Christ is the firstfruits, He has guaranteed the whole harvest. The sheaf that was brought to the priest was exactly like the harvest in the field. It would have been a barley sheaf, identical to the grain in the field. One day we shall be like the Lord Jesus Christ! The fact that Jesus Christ is the firstfruits assures us that we shall be like Him. One day we shall have a body like His glorious body (Phil. 3:20,21). We know, "When he shall appear, we shall be like him; for we shall see him as he is" (I John 3:2).

Christ is the One who established the Lord's Day, the first day of the week. For centuries the Jews labored for six days and then rested. But the New Testament Christian *first* finds his rest in Jesus Christ (on the first day of the week), and *then* he labors for Him. The Sabbath Day is a picture of

44

salvation by works. The Lord's Day is a picture of salvation by grace.

When is this harvest going to take place? Nobody knows. We do not know when our Lord Jesus is going to come back. But when He comes, He will reap His glorious harvest. "Every man in his own order: Christ the firstfruits; afterward they that are Christ's at his coming" (I Cor. 15:23). The resurrection of Christ assures us that the dead in Christ shall be raised.

The Bible teaches that there are two resurrections. There is the first resurrection, which is a resurrection unto life and blessing; and there is a second resurrection, which is a resurrection unto death and condemnation (Rev. 20:1-6; John 11:25,26; 5:24-29). If you have trusted Christ as your Saviour, then you will participate in that wonderful first resurrection when Jesus Christ shall come for His people.

Did you note that the people were not permitted to eat the grain until they had first given the sheaf to the Lord? Jesus said, "My meat [my food] is to do the will of him that sent me, and to finish his work" (John 4:34). Put Him first in your life; give Him first place in your life. Make the will of God the nourishment of your soul.

Jesus Christ is alive today. He is the firstfruits. When He returns, He will take home to Himself those who have trusted Him as their Saviour. I hope you have trusted Him and know that He is the firstfruits. And I trust that you and I are giving Him first place in our lives. We must give Him the firstfruits of all that He gives to us, the very best that we have. After all, He has given His all for us.

The Assurance of Heaven

Another practical lesson that we can learn from this Feast of Firstfruits is that *we have the assurance of heaven.* We know we are going to heaven because the Holy Spirit is "the firstfruits" in the life of the believer. "For we know that the whole creation groaneth and travaileth in pain together until now. And not only they, but ourselves also, which have the firstfruits of the Spirit, even we ourselves groan within ourselves, waiting for the adoption, to wit [that is], the redemption of our body" (Rom. 8:22,23).

In Romans 8, Paul was writing about victory, explaining how the Christian can walk in victory. Paul admitted that there is suffering in this world. Some religious groups deny the existence of suffering, but Paul declared just the opposite. He affirmed that there is suffering in this world. "For I reckon that the sufferings of this present time are not worthy to be compared with the glory which shall be revealed in us" (v. 18). God does not *take away* suffering; rather, He *transforms* suffering. The suffering that we endure today is going to turn to glory when Jesus Christ comes back. All of creation is groaning and travailing in pain. This, of course, is the result of sin. When will this travail end? When Jesus Christ returns. We Christians are waiting, along with creation, for "the adoption, to wit, the redemption of our body" (v. 23). When you trusted

Christ as your Saviour, your spirit was redeemed and you were set free from the guilt and penalty of sin. As you walk with the Lord, you experience even greater freedom—the freedom of obedience, the freedom of glorifying God. But one of these days *the body* is going to be redeemed!

Today God is not specializing in redeeming bodies. He does heal bodies in answer to prayer, but that is not His main work today. His main work is saving souls and making people more like Christ. But when Jesus comes, we will be changed. We read in Philippians 3:20,21: "Our conversation [citizenship] is in heaven; from whence also we look for the Saviour, the Lord Jesus Christ: who shall change our vile body, that it may be fashioned like unto his glorious body."

Meanwhile, what do we do? Is this just "pie in the sky by and by"? Is this some sort of a religious sedative that we take? When we are suffering, when we are going through difficulty, do we pacify ourselves by saying, "Well, the Lord's going to come back someday, and so I'll look ahead"? There is more to it than that!

The Firstfruits of the Spirit

Romans 8:23 tells us that we have the firstfruits of the Spirit right now! We're told in II Corinthians 1:21,22 that the Holy Spirit has sealed us and is the earnest of our inheritance. In Bible times, when you purchased something, you put your seal on it and nobody would touch it. It belonged to you. So the Holy Spirit is God's seal in our lives to the day of redemption. He is the down payment, the earnest. The Holy Spirit has been given to us as the guarantee that the rest is going to follow.

The "firstfruits of the Spirit" simply means that the Holy Spirit in us today is the beginning of the harvest. Many of us are enjoying (I trust) "the fruit of the Spirit," not just the "firstfruits of the Spirit." The fruit of the Spirit is described in Galatians 5:22,23: "Love, joy, peace" and that whole beautiful cluster of spiritual graces.

The firstfruits of the Spirit simply means that what the Holy Spirit is doing *now* is a foretaste of heaven to come! Some Christians do not have a good relationship with the Holy Spirit. This is unfortunate, because the Holy Spirit wants to bring heaven to your life right now. Charles Spurgeon used to say, "Little faith will take your soul to heaven, but great faith will bring heaven to your soul." The Lord Jesus has not returned yet. We are not in heaven yet. We are going through times of suffering and difficulty with problems and concerns. What is the answer? The answer is the firstfruits of the Spirit. The Holy Spirit lives in the life of each believer, and the Spirit wants to give you a foretaste of heaven today.

You and I are looking forward to going to heaven. (It doesn't mean we're going to hasten the process by not taking care of ourselves, because that would be sinning.) We are looking forward to Jesus' coming back and taking us to Himself. We see so much trouble and turmoil in this world. You may say, "Your attitude is escapist!" I don't think it is. While I am in this world, I am enjoying the firstfruits of the Spirit. The Holy Spirit glorifies Christ, so today we can experience the glory of Christ. The Holy Spirit enables us to praise and worship God. We will worship and praise the Lord in heaven, but the Holy Spirit enables us to do it *now*. The Holy Spirit teaches us God's Word and enables us to grow in Christian character.

Some people have the idea that, no matter how they lived as a Christian, when they die and go to heaven, they will be just like the spiritual giants of the faith. But that idea is not true. An old Puritan preacher used to say, "Every vessel in heaven will be filled, but some vessels will be larger than others." Why will some vessels be larger than others? Because those people walked with the Lord and enjoyed the firstfruits of the Spirit here on earth. You and I need to prepare right now for the blessings of heaven.

The Holy Spirit enables us to fellowship with God's people. The love of the Holy Spirit draws us together. In heaven we are going to fellowship together, so start enjoying it now! There may be somebody in your church you don't want to talk to, so you bypass him and avoid him. Well, you won't avoid him in heaven! We must learn to get along with each other here on earth, and the Holy Spirit helps us.

The Holy Spirit gives us a foretaste of heaven. He is "the firstfruits" of heaven in our lives. As you walk with the Lord and as the Holy Spirit ministers to

49

you, you enjoy heaven on earth. This experience makes it possible for us to overcome suffering and pain, bereavement and trial. Instead of complaining, we rejoice and look forward to seeing all of this suffering one day turned into glory.

Believers As the Firstfruits

Finally, you and I as believers are a part of the firstfruits. "Likewise greet the church that is in their house. [The assemblies in Rome met in various house groups.] Salute my well-beloved Epaenetus, who is the firstfruits of Achaia [Asia] unto Christ" (Rom. 16:5). Did you know that when you were saved, you became firstfruits? "Of his own will begat he us with the word of truth, that we should be a kind of firstfruits of his creatures" (James 1:18). What does this mean? It means that you are the beginning of the harvest. Paul won Epaenetus to Christ, and Epaenetus became the firstfruits of Asia. He was the beginning of the harvest, and he assisted Paul in winning other people to the Saviour.

You and I were saved that we might increase the harvest. Our Lord Jesus met a needy woman at the well of Sychar one day, and she trusted him for salvation (see John 4). She became the firstfruits. She went back into the city, bore witness of her faith in Christ, and the whole city turned out to hear the Lord Jesus! Many of them trusted Him as Saviour. They begged Him to stay and teach them more of the Word of God. That unnamed woman was the firstfruits; she was the beginning of the harvest.

50

You may say, "I am the only believer in my family." Well, that is an opportunity, isn't it? You are the firstfruits—*the harvest ought to follow!* Perhaps you are the only believer in your factory, office or school. Again, that is an opportunity for you. You are the firstfruits. And the harvest is supposed to follow.

The thing for us to do is just to give ourselves to the Lord and let Him use us. The Old Testament priest took the firstfruits and waved them unto the Lord in dedication. We ought to give ourselves to the Lord and say, "Lord, I'm just the firstfruits. There are no other Christians in my office or my family or my school. Please help me to be a witness that I might win others. I want to be the firstfruits leading to the harvest." "He that goeth forth and weepeth, bearing precious seed, shall doubtless come again with rejoicing, bringing his sheaves with him" (Ps. 126:6).

I know it is not easy to be the only Christian in your office or on your campus or in your neighborhood. It is not easy, but it is a great opportunity to see God work in and through you to bring a harvest.

This, then, is the meaning of the Feast of the Firstfruits. God deserves our very best. Give Him the first and the best—not the leftovers. Jesus Christ has been raised from the dead; He is the firstfruits of them that slept, and one day He shall return and claim His harvest. The dead in Christ shall be raised, and we shall be together with the Lord. The Holy Spirit is the firstfruits of heaven. In our heart we can enjoy the blessings of heaven

51

today. You and I as believers are the firstfruits, and God is looking for a harvest.

Be God's guest! He invites you to days of heaven on earth!

Chapter 6

Pentecost: The Comforter Is Come!

The Feast of Pentecost is the fourth of the special feasts recorded in Leviticus 23. Fifty days following Firstfruits, the Feast of Pentecost occurred. "And ye shall count unto you from the morrow after the sabbath, from the day that ye brought the sheaf of the wave-offering; seven sabbaths shall be complete: even unto the morrow after the seventh sabbath shall ye number fifty days; [the word "Pentecost" means 50] and ye shall offer a new meat-offering [meal-offering] unto the Lord" (vv. 15,16).

You will notice that Pentecost occurred on the 50th day, which would put it on the first day of the week, the Lord's Day. Firstfruits and Pentecost both occurred on the first day of the week. For Christians, this is the Lord's Day. The Feast of Firstfruits commemorates our Lord's resurrection from the dead, and the Feast of Pentecost commemorates the coming of the Holy Spirit. By His resurrection and by His sending of the Holy Spirit, our Lord has consecrated the first day of the week in a very special way.

You will also notice that the priest was to offer a

new meal-offering (see Lev. 23:16). Pentecost brought into the world something new—the Church. God had always had His people on this earth, but the Church is a very special people. Jesus said, "I will build my church" (Matt. 16:18).

"Ye shall bring out of your habitations two wave-loaves of two tenth deals [parts]" (Lev. 23:17). It goes on to explain that the loaves would be made of fine flour, *baked with leaven*. This is rather interesting because the Jews were not to bring their offerings *with leaven*. We discovered that leaven is a picture of sin, and yet these two loaves were to be baked with leaven! Why? Because the loaves picture the Church, and there is sin in the Church. Not until the Church arrives in heaven will it be sinless. How can God accept a sinful people? On the basis of the sacrifice of Christ, illustrated in the many sacrifices named in Leviticus 23:18,19. These sacrifices picture the work of our Lord Jesus Christ on the cross. The burnt-offering pictures complete consecration—He gave Himself completely. The sin-offering, of course, speaks of our Lord Jesus dying for our sins. And the peace-offering—the fact that Jesus, through His death, has made peace with God.

The fulfillment of all of this is recorded in Acts 2 when the Holy Spirit came at Pentecost. If you put together Acts 2 and Leviticus 23, you will learn some beautiful lessons about the Holy Spirit. Four activities of the Spirit are recorded in Acts 2.

First of all, *the Holy Spirit came.* Then the Holy

Spirit *baptized*. Third, the Holy Spirit *filled*. Fourth, the Holy Spirit *spoke*.

"And when the day of Pentecost was fully come, they [the apostles and the other believers] were all with one accord in one place. And suddenly there came a sound from heaven as of a rushing mighty wind, and it filled all the house where they were sitting. And there appeared unto them cloven tongues like as of fire, and it sat upon each of them. And they were all filled with the Holy Ghost [Spirit], and began to speak with other tongues, as the Spirit gave them utterance" (Acts 2:1-4).

The Spirit Came

On the Day of Pentecost, *the Spirit came*. This does not mean that the Holy Spirit had not ministered on earth before Pentecost. The Holy Spirit worked in creation. "The Spirit of God moved upon the face of the waters" (Gen. 1:2). The Spirit of God empowered men of God to serve Him. The Holy Spirit came upon different men of God—judges and kings, warriors and workers—to accomplish His purposes. Of course, the Holy Spirit had worked in the life of Christ. The Holy Spirit had conceived the body of Christ in the womb of Mary. The Holy Spirit had anointed and empowered the Lord Jesus for His ministry on earth. When our Lord preached in Nazareth, He said, "The Spirit of the Lord is upon me, because he hath anointed me to preach the gospel to the poor" (Luke 4:18).

So the Holy Spirit had ministered in creation, in the history of the Jewish nation and in the life of the

Lord Jesus Christ. But now the Holy Spirit was going to come in a new and special way.

"And I will pray the Father, and he shall give you another Comforter, that he may abide with you for ever; even the Spirit of truth; whom the world cannot receive, because it seeth him not, neither knoweth him: but ye know him; for he dwelleth with you, and shall be in you" (John 14:16,17). The Holy Spirit had dwelt *with* the apostles in the Person of Jesus Christ. But after Pentecost, the Spirit would live *in* them. Furthermore, this dwelling would be *permanent,* not temporary.

In the Old Testament age, the Holy Spirit had come upon men *temporarily* to accomplish a special work, and then He would depart. For example, the Holy Spirit empowered King Saul, but when Saul sinned against God, God removed the Holy Spirit. This explains why David prayed in Psalm 51, "Take not thy holy spirit from me" (v. 11).

We don't pray that way today because God will not take His Holy Spirit from us. Jesus said, "And I will pray the Father, and he shall give you another Comforter, that he may abide with you for ever" (John 14:16).

Keep in mind, then, these two special truths. First, the Holy Spirit would *indwell* people, not just come upon them. Second, the Holy Spirit would be a *permanent* resident, not a temporary visitor. You may ask, "Why didn't the Holy Spirit do all of this sooner?" Because God has His calendar. The explanation is given in John 7:37,38.

"In the last day, that great day of the feast, Jesus

stood and cried, saying, If any man thirst, let him come unto me, and drink. He that believeth on me, as the scripture hath said, out of his belly [innermost being] shall flow rivers of living water." Now, here's the explanation: "(But this spake he of the Spirit, which they that believe on him should receive: for the Holy Ghost was not yet given; because that Jesus was not yet glorified)" (v. 39). You see, God has His timetable. First, Passover—the Lamb was slain. Then the Lamb was raised from the dead—that's the Feast of Firstfruits. Now, 50 days later, the glorified Lamb of God sends the Holy Spirit. He could not send the Holy Spirit until He was glorified, and of course, He could not be glorified until He was crucified. His glorification involved being crucified and buried, being raised from the dead and then ascending back to heaven that He might send the Holy Spirit. The Holy Spirit came, and He came right on schedule.

The Spirit Baptized

Now, second, *the Holy Spirit baptized.* We hear a great deal these days about "the baptism of the Holy Spirit." We must get our facts from the Bible, not from men's experience. We read in Acts 1:4,5: "And, being assembled together with them, [Jesus] commanded them that they should not depart from Jerusalem, but wait for the promise of the Father, which, saith he, ye have heard of me. For John [John the Baptist] truly baptized with water; but ye shall be baptized with the Holy Ghost not many days hence." This promise of the baptism of the

57

Holy Spirit is found in Matthew, Mark, Luke, John and Acts. John the Baptist announced that the Lord Jesus Christ, who was greater than John, would baptize with the Holy Spirit.

Please notice that Jesus said nothing about the baptism of fire. John the Baptist had said, "He shall baptize you with the Holy Ghost, and with fire" (Matt. 3:11). My own personal conviction is that the "baptism of fire" is a future baptism of judgment that is going to come upon this earth to those who have rejected the Saviour. Our Lord said nothing in Acts 1 about a baptism of fire, but He did talk about the Holy Spirit's baptizing the believers. This baptism of the Spirit must be important, or it would not be found in all four Gospels and also in the Book of the Acts.

The word "baptize" has a twofold meaning. There is a literal meaning and a figurative meaning. Many words in our language have both literal and figurative meanings. We say that someone is "going through the waters." Well, that could mean he is wading out in a trout stream or that he is going through times of difficulty. You see, there is a literal meaning, and there is a figurative meaning.

Now, *literally,* the word "baptize" means "to submerge, to immerse." But *figuratively* it means "to be identified with." When the Holy Spirit came at Pentecost, He identified the believers with their glorified Head, the Lord Jesus, and formed the body, which is the Church. Now, this truth is amplified in I Corinthians 12:13: "For by one Spirit are we all baptized into one body, whether we be Jews or Gentiles,

58

whether we be bond or free." The Spirit of God formed the body of Jesus Christ on earth—the Church—when He came at Pentecost. Of course, there had already been individual believers on earth, but they had not yet been formed into a spiritual unity. Now they were united into one Body.

So the Spirit baptized. This meant that the believers were united in a spiritual unity, identified with their glorified Saviour in heaven. This helps us understand why the priest brought two wave-loaves. You see, at Firstfruits they brought a sheaf—individual grains; but at Pentecost, these grains had been ground, they had been made into flour, they had been baked into two loaves. The loaves speak of the corporate body—the Church— not individual grains but grains united to each other.

I meet believers who say, "Oh, I can be a good Christian without the Church." I want you to know you are a part of the Church whether you like it or not. When you were saved, you were baptized by the Spirit of God into the Body of Christ. And whether or not you meet in a local assembly, you are still a part of the Body of Christ, and you *ought* to meet with other believers to worship, to witness, to work and to glorify the Lord.

But why did the priest bring *two* loaves? Because believing *Jews* were baptized into the Body of Christ at Pentecost (Acts 2), and in Acts 10 believing *Gentiles* were baptized into the Body of Christ. "To the Jew first" is God's program. There was one baptism by the Spirit, but it took place on two different occasions.

Why was there leaven in these loaves? Because there is sin in the Church. The Church is not perfect. God recognizes this fact and encourages us to purify our lives. But some professing Christians stay away from the church because the church is not perfect. You have heard the old saying: "Well, I'm not going to go to church—there are hypocrites in the church!" The answer, of course, is "Well, there's room for one more!" No one is perfect. The Church is made up of imperfect people on their way to heaven.

At Pentecost, the Church was born when the Spirit came and baptized believers. You and I are a part of that wonderful fellowship because we have trusted Christ as our Saviour.

The Spirit Filled

The third activity of the Holy Spirit at Pentecost is found in Acts 2:4: "And they were all filled with the Holy Ghost." The Holy Spirit came, the Holy Spirit baptized, and *the Holy Spirit filled.*

The classic text on the fullness of the Spirit is Ephesians 5:18: "And be not drunk with wine, wherein is excess; but be filled with the Spirit." Never confuse the baptism of the Spirit with the filling of the Spirit. I've heard preachers say, "Oh, it makes no difference what you call it as long as you have the experience." I don't believe that for one minute. If I go to my doctor, I want him to use the right terminology. If there's something wrong with my gall bladder, I don't want him talking about my lungs or my liver. Bible terminology is accurate, and we do not have the privilege or the right to change the words that God has written, inspired by the Holy Spirit (see I Cor. 2:12,13).

The baptism of the Holy Spirit happens once. The Holy Spirit came down at Pentecost and baptized the Jews into the Body of Christ and later baptized the Gentiles into the Body of Christ. When you were saved, the same Spirit baptized you into the Body of Christ. There is no repetition of the baptism of the Spirit.

There is, however, a repetition of the *fullness* of the Spirit. In the Book of the Acts you read that the believers were repeatedly filled with the Spirit (Acts 2:4; 4:8,31). We do not read that they were repeatedly baptized by the Spirit.

Nowhere in the Bible are we commanded to be baptized by the Spirit of God. But we are commanded to be filled (see Eph. 5:18). The fullness of the Holy Spirit requires our cooperation. The baptism of the Spirit occurs when you trust Christ as your Saviour, once and for all. The baptism of the Spirit is a *single* experience. The fullness is a repeated experience. We are commanded to be filled. We are not commanded to be baptized. The baptism of the Spirit is a *collective* experience. It puts me into the Body of Christ. The fullness of the Spirit is a personal, individual experience, giving the believer power for witness and for Christian living.

Why were the apostles and the other believers filled with the Holy Spirit? Primarily that they might witness by word and by deed. Acts 1:8 makes that very clear. The task of the Church is witnessing. We

61

are all commanded to be witnesses, and we should seek to win as many as we can. Witnessing is the work of the Holy Spirit through the believer. Some people have a very special gift of soul winning. They are able to lead people to Christ easily because they have a gift. Not every Christian can reap the harvest, but all can sow the seed. If we are filled with the Spirit of God, we can bear witness of our Lord Jesus Christ.

Now, how do you know if you are filled with the Holy Spirit? Ephesians 5 tells us, in verses 19 and following, that we will be *joyful:* "Speaking to yourselves in psalms and hymns and spiritual songs, singing and making melody in your heart to the Lord." We will be *thankful:* "Giving thanks always for all things unto God in the Father in the name of our Lord Jesus Christ." And we will be *submissive:* "Submitting yourselves one to another in the fear of God." When you are filled with the Holy Spirit, you find it easy to remember Scripture, because the Holy Spirit reminds you. When you are filled with the Spirit, you have a desire to witness, and the witness comes from God. It's not something you manufacture.

The Spirit filled these believers, and because they were filled with the Holy Spirit, they went forth giving bold witness for the Lord. "But ye shall receive power, after that the Holy Ghost is come upon you: and ye shall be witnesses unto me," promised the Lord Jesus in Acts 1:8. We need this today.

I preached in a church recently where, before the service, the elders of the church knelt in prayer. They prayed for the fullness of the Holy Spirit, that all who were sharing in the ministry of the Word might have power to bear witness to Jesus Christ. We had a wonderful service!

To be filled with the Holy Spirit requires cleansing. We must confess our sins and be cleansed by the blood of Jesus Christ. We must want to be filled for the glory of God—not to enjoy a selfish experience.

The Spirit Spoke

The fourth activity of the Holy Spirit is also recorded in Acts 2:4—*the Holy Spirit spoke.* "They all were filled with the Holy Ghost, and began to speak with other tongues, as the Spirit gave them utterance." The men were not controlling the Holy Spirit—the Spirit was controlling these men. When you are baptized by the Holy Spirit, you belong to Christ's Body. When you are filled with the Holy Spirit, your body belongs to Him. Then He can work through you.

This whole subject of tongues has created many problems for people. If you will read Acts 2 very carefully, you will discover, first of all, that they were *praising God* in tongues—they were not preaching. The believers were sharing with the people "the wonderful works of God" (v. 11). The tongues were used for the purpose of praising God. Second, when Peter stood up to preach, he preached in the Hebrew language, not in tongues. So keep in mind that the gift of tongues at Pentecost was for the

63

purpose of praising God and bearing witness of what He had done, not for preaching the gospel.

Something else is true: These tongues were *known languages*. There are 16 different geographical places mentioned in Acts 2:7-11. "Every man heard them speak in his own language" (v. 6). The Greek word translated "language" gives us our English word "dialect." They heard them speaking in their own language. They asked, "And how hear we every man in our own tongue, wherein we were born?" (v. 8).

The believers did not speak in some "heavenly language." They did not use some brand-new language. The Holy Spirit used the tongues of believers to praise God in languages *that were already in use*.

The gift of tongues is not an evidence of either the baptism of the Spirit or the fullness of the Spirit. Nowhere do we find this in Scripture. When I was converted, I was baptized instantly by the Holy Spirit into the Body of Christ. I did not speak in tongues, but I want you to know I was soundly converted. The Spirit of God came into my life and bore witness to me that I was a child of God.

The baptism of the Spirit is not evidenced by tongues nor is the fullness of the Spirit. There are multitudes of believers who have been filled with the Holy Spirit and served in great power, yet they have never spoken in tongues.

Nor are tongues an evidence of spiritual maturity. The church at Corinth had a great deal of speaking in tongues, and yet they were very immature, worldly and carnal. Don't let anyone confuse you. If someone says, "If you are baptized by the Spirit, you must speak in tongues," do not believe him. You were baptized by the Spirit when you were saved. If they say, "Well, if you are filled with the Spirit, then you will speak in tongues," that statement is not biblical. Not everyone is going to have a gift of tongues. In fact, I Corinthians 12:30 makes this very clear. "Do all speak with tongues?" Paul asked. And the answer is, according to the structure of the Greek, no. Not everybody speaks in tongues.

Paul tells us in I Corinthians 12, 13 and 14 how this gift of tongues was supposed to be used. Some people have asked me, "Do you think God could give the gift of tongues today?" I think God is sovereign, and God can do whatever He wants to do. There are those who believe that this gift was removed and cannot come back. I understand their position, but I don't necessarily defend it. I do not believe that every believer has to speak in tongues. I do believe that God can, if He wants to, give a gift of tongues. But we must not make this a test of anything.

There are some people who have had a false experience—a counterfeit experience. Not everybody who thinks he is filled with the Spirit is really filled with the Spirit. He might be fooled by the spirits! Satan is a great counterfeiter. We must exercise spiritual discernment.

The Spirit of God can use your tongue to praise God and to witness to the lost. Sad to say, some people have their tongues set on fire from hell (see

James 3:6). There are Christians who go around gossiping and criticizing, creating problems in their family and in their church. Their tongue is "set on fire of hell." The apostles had their tongues set on fire from heaven, and they gave powerful witness to Jesus Christ. When Peter preached the gospel, filled with the Spirit, God used his tongue, and 3000 people came to know Christ as their Saviour.

The important thing is that we are filled with the Spirit of God. The Spirit of God has come—that is a settled matter. The Spirit of God has baptized believers into the Church—that, too, is a settled matter. The Spirit of God can fill us, moment by moment, and enable us to glorify God. The Spirit of God can speak through us in languages people understand.

Has your tongue been set on fire from heaven? It is not important that you have some miraculous ecstatic experience. It is important that the Holy Spirit use you to bear witness to Jesus Christ and to share the gospel with the whole world.

Chapter 7

Trumpets: God's Scattered People

The first four feasts that are given in Leviticus 23
describe for us the *past* work that God has done.
The Passover—Christ died for our sins. The Feast
of Unleavened Bread—what Christ did enables us
to cleanse our lives, to feast upon Him and to have
the spiritual sustenance that we need for our pilgrim
journey. The Feast of Firstfruits—the resurrection
of our Lord Jesus Christ. Fifty days later was the
Feast of Pentecost—the coming of the Holy Spirit.

These four feasts picture events in past history.
We are living between the Feast of Pentecost and
the Feast of Trumpets. There is a three-month gap
in the Jewish calendar between the Feast of Pentecost (third month) and the Feast of Trumpets (seventh month).

What were the Jewish people doing during that
time? They were sharing in the harvest. Pentecost
was a harvest feast. The people were working in the
harvest field. This is what you and I should be doing
today.

After Moses described the Feast of Pentecost in
Leviticus 23:15-21, he immediately talked about the

67

harvest: "And when ye reap the harvest of your land" (v. 22). You and I today are a part of the harvest. Sad to say, many people are *watching* the harvest or *neglecting* the harvest. Our Lord tells us that "they [the fields] are white already to harvest" (John 4:35). It is not our job to be criticizing the harvesters or painting pictures of the harvest. Our job is to be out helping to bring in the sheaves. Are you a part of the harvest crew today?

The next event on God's calendar is the Feast of Trumpets on the first day of the seventh month. "Speak unto the children of Israel, saying, In the seventh month, in the first day of the month, shall ye have a sabbath, a memorial of blowing of trumpets, an holy convocation. Ye shall do no servile work therein: but ye shall offer an offering made by fire unto the Lord" (Lev. 23:24,25).

The nation of Israel was all "wrapped up" in *sevens*. On the seventh *day* of the week was the Sabbath. There are seven *feasts* of Jehovah. Seven *weeks* after Firstfruits is Pentecost. After the seven *years* was the Sabbatical year. Seven times seven— 49 years—introduces the year of Jubilee. In Daniel 9 seven times 70—490 years—describes God's prophetic plan for Israel. In the seventh month there were three very important feasts: Trumpets, the Day of Atonement and Tabernacles.

The four feasts we have already discussed deal with what God has already done for the salvation of lost souls. The next three feasts describe what God will do in the future. Their application is *basically* to the nation of Israel, but there is still a spiritual and

68

prophetic meaning for those of us who belong to the Church.

The Feast of Trumpets speaks of the time when our Lord Jesus shall return and take us to be with Him. The Day of Atonement reminds me of that time when I am going to stand before the Judgment Seat of Christ. It shall be a time of cleansing and a time of rewarding. The Feast of Tabernacles speaks of the wonderful, joyful time we will have sharing in the blessings of the kingdom with our Saviour.

For Israel

For the nation of Israel these three feasts have a very definite application because Israel has a three-fold problem. Israel is a scattered people, a sinful people and a suffering people. Israel is a scattered people because Israel did not obey God. We are told in Deuteronomy 28 and Leviticus 26 about the scattering of the people of Israel. The Feast of Trumpets speaks of a time of gathering, when God shall call His scattered people together.

Israel is a sinful people. All of us are sinners. Jews are not greater sinners than Gentiles. But Israel sinned against a flood of light and against a wealth of privileges. The Day of Atonement speaks of that time when Israel shall be cleansed and born again.

So the scattered people shall be called, and the sinful people shall be cleansed, and the suffering people shall be comforted. The Feast of Tabernacles speaks of that time when God shall give His people the kingdom that He promised in the Old Testament prophecies.

In Numbers 10, God gives an explanation concerning the use of the trumpets. Israel used the trumpets for very important purposes. The trumpets were used for calling the assembly. "Make thee two trumpets of silver; of a whole piece shalt thou make them: that thou mayest use them for the calling of the assembly, and for the journeying of the camps" (v. 2). The trumpets were also used to blow an alarm (v. 5) and to announce war (v. 9). The trumpets were used to announce the special days in the calendar of Israel—the solemn feasts and the sacrifices and so forth (v. 10).

The trumpets were God's method of communication. They were God's telephone, God's radio, God's newspaper. When God wanted to announce something to His people or get His people to do something, then He told the priests to blow the trumpets.

Israel is a scattered people. Israel should be dwelling in her land and enjoying all the blessings of the land. There are people who have returned to Palestine, as we know. I can remember, early in my Christian life, reading books that said there was no future for Israel, either politically or spiritually. And yet the nation of Israel is back on the map again—that great miracle took place back in 1948. Israel is at the center of the stage in the Middle East. We see some of the people returning to the land, but Israel is still a scattered people. They are scattered because they disobeyed God.

Let me make it very clear that all men have disobeyed God. "All have sinned, and come short of the glory of God" (Rom. 3:23). No one nation is purer than any other nation. But Israel had so many privileges. God gave to Israel the patriarchs, the prophets, the covenants, the temple, the priesthood, the sacrifices and the great promise of the Messiah. And yet Israel did not live up to her privileges. She rebelled against God, and God had to punish her.

First, God punished Israel *in the land.* In the Book of Judges it is recorded that seven nations came into the land to punish disobedient Israel. Then when the nation continued to disobey, God took them *out of the land* and "spanked" them. He took them off into Babylonian Captivity, and after 70 years, He permitted them to return. When they sinned once again and rejected the Messiah, He scattered them across the world.

Israel is a scattered people, but the Feast of Trumpets speaks of a time when God will gather His people back to the land and save them.

"And it shall come to pass in that day, that the Lord shall beat off from the channel of the river unto the stream of Egypt, and ye shall be gathered one by one, O ye children of Israel. And it shall come to pass in that day, that the great trumpet shall be blown, and they shall come which were ready to perish in the land of Assyria, and the outcasts in the land of Egypt, and shall worship the Lord in the holy mount at Jerusalem" (Isa. 27:12,13).

Read the Book of Joel, and you will find several references to that future "day of the Lord," when the trumpet will be blown. Joel 2:1 says, "Blow ye the trumpet in Zion, and sound an alarm in my holy mountain." We read in Joel 2:15: "Blow the trumpet in Zion, sanctify a fast, call a solemn assembly." Joel is talking about the time when the people of Israel shall be gathered together and God shall bring them back to the land and restore them to their kingdom.

One day there will be a great "blowing of the trumpet" for the nation of Israel. In His great prophetic sermon called "the Olivet Discourse" (Matt. 24,25), Jesus said, "Immediately after the tribulation of those days shall the sun be darkened, and the moon shall not give her light, and the stars shall fall from heaven, and the powers of the heavens shall be shaken. . . . And he shall send his angels with a great sound of a trumpet, and they shall gather together his elect from the four winds, from one end of heaven to the other" (24:29,31).

So Israel shall be regathered. There will be a time of cleansing and restoration.

For the Church

As far as the Church is concerned, there will be the sounding of a trumpet for us as well. The Church is also a scattered people. Some of God's people are on earth—scattered from one place to another—and some are in heaven. Christ will assemble His people and take them to heaven (I Thess. 4:13-18). Let me make it very clear that the Feast of Trumpets in its *basic interpretation* belongs to Israel. But in its personal application, there is a message for us as Christians. "For this we say unto you by the word of the Lord, that we which are alive

72

and remain unto the coming of the Lord shall not prevent [precede] them which are asleep. For the Lord himself shall descend from heaven with a shout, with the voice of the archangel, and with the trump of God: and the dead in Christ shall rise first" (vv. 15,16). "For the trumpet shall sound, and the dead shall be raised incorruptible" (I Cor. 15:52).

The trumpets were blown in Israel to gather the people together, to move the people forward and to give the alarm for war. When the trumpet sounds from heaven, Christ will gather His Church together, take them to glory and, at the same time, sound the alarm of war. "For when they shall say, Peace and safety; then sudden destruction cometh upon them, as travail upon a woman with child; and they shall not escape" (I Thess. 5:3). When God calls His Church home from this world, He will then declare war on the world and send such tribulation as people have never seen before.

We are waiting for the sound of the trumpet. As we labor in the harvest, the thing that keeps us going is that Jesus is coming again. As we wait and as we witness and as we work, we know that He is going to come again and take us to heaven. "Lift up your heads; for your redemption draweth nigh" (Luke 21:28). Jesus is coming again! Let's be faithful to serve Him today!

Be God's guest! One day the trumpet will sound!

Chapter 8

Day of Atonement: Seven Appointments

The Books of Genesis through Deuteronomy form the foundation for the Bible. In these books we have the record of how the world began, how man began, how man sinned, what sin has done in the world and how God has called His people to salvation.

The heart of Genesis through Deuteronomy is Leviticus. This book describes the sacrifices and the work of the priesthood. That little tent in the middle of the camp of Israel was the center of God's working in the world. There the sacrifices were brought, and there the priests offered them to God.

But the heart of Leviticus is chapter 16—the Day of Atonement. On the tenth day of the seventh month everything in the camp of Israel ceased. No work was done, no burden was lifted. Only one man was busy, and that man was the high priest. There are seven very important *appointments* in Leviticus 16 where the Day of Atonement is described.

An Appointed Purpose

First of all, there was *an appointed purpose*. What was the reason behind all of the ritual and sacrifice that took place on the Day of Atonement? Leviticus 16:30 tells us: "For on that day shall the priest make an atonement for you, to cleanse you, that ye may be clean from all your sins before the Lord." Our Jewish friends call this Yom Kippur, the Day of Atonement.

The word "atonement" is used 15 times in Leviticus 16. Among other things the Hebrew word means "to cover." Under the Old Testament economy, the blood of the sacrifices could not put away sin; it could only cover sin. The blood of bulls and goats could not take away sin; it could only cover sin. Only Jesus Christ's blood can take away sin (John 1:29).

The problem that God has to solve is the problem of sin. God is holy and man is sinful. Everything in the camp of Israel had been defiled by sin. Leviticus 16:33 says, "And he shall make an atonement for the holy sanctuary, and he shall make an atonement for the tabernacle of the congregation, and for the altar, and he shall make an atonement for the priests, and for all the people of the congregation." Even the holy tabernacle of God and the priesthood had been defiled by sin. Of course, the people were also defiled by their sins.

Leviticus 16:21 describes the different kinds of sins the people had committed. They had committed *iniquities, transgressions* and *sins*. "Iniquity" means crookedness—we are twisted out of shape and do not measure up to God's standard. "Transgression" means rebellion—to cross over the line

75

and go too far. The word "sin" means to miss the mark—to err from our appointed goal. The appointed purpose was to deal with the problem of sin. The heart of every problem is the problem in the heart, and the problem in the heart is sin.

An Appointed Time

Second, there was *an appointed time*. The priest did not do this every day of the week; he did this once a year. "Speak unto Aaron thy brother, that he come not at all times into the holy place within the vail before the mercy seat, which is upon the ark; that he die not: for I will appear in the cloud upon the mercy seat" (Lev. 16:2).

Once a year the high priest was allowed to go into the Holy of Holies. Every year this ceremony had to be repeated because the sacrifices could not take away sin. Our Lord Jesus Christ finished the work once and for all. One of the basic themes of the Book of Hebrews is the fact that Jesus Christ has accomplished a finished salvation. "For Christ is not entered into the holy places made with hands, which are the figures of the true; but into heaven itself, now to appear in the presence of God for us: nor yet that he should offer himself often, as the high priest entereth into the holy place every year with blood of others; . . . but now once in the end of the world hath he appeared to put away sin by the sacrifice of himself" (9:24-26).

An Appointed Place

Third, there was *an appointed place*. God had appointed only one place of sacrifice. Leviticus 17 makes it very clear that there is but one place of sacrifice: The tabernacle (and later on the temple) was God's appointed place. There is only one appointed place of sacrifice as far as salvation is concerned—the cross where Jesus died. "Who his own self bare our sins in his own body on the tree" (I Pet. 2:24). Our Lord did not bear our sins in the Jordan River when he was baptized. Baptism is not the way of salvation. Our Lord did not bear our sins in the temple as He was teaching. Education, as good as it is, is not God's way of salvation. Christ bore our sins at the appointed place—the cross.

An Appointed Person

Fourth, there was an appointed person. Not everyone was permitted to offer this sacrifice—only the high priest. "And there shall be no man in the tabernacle of the congregation when he goeth in to make an atonement in the holy place, until he come out" (Lev. 16:17). In other words, the high priest had to fulfill this responsibility alone. First, he put off his beautiful garments. Then he washed his flesh in water (v. 4) and put on the plain linen garments of a lowly servant.

This is a picture, of course, of our Lord Jesus. There came a time when He laid aside His beautiful garments of glory. He attired Himself in the garments of a servant. He set Himself apart to do the will of God. He came to earth and was obedient unto death. God's appointed person for today is the Lord Jesus Christ, our glorified High Priest in

77

heaven. The Old Testament high priest had to offer sacrifices first for himself before he could offer sacrifices for the people. Jesus needed no sacrifices for Himself, for He was holy, harmless, undefiled, separate from sinners. Instead, He offered Himself as the sinless sacrifice.

An Appointed Price

Fifth, there was *an appointed price to pay,* and that price was blood. Eighty-six times in the Book of Leviticus the blood is mentioned. It was not living animals that paid the price; it was dead animals offered as sacrifices. The blood had to be shed. Some people reject this teaching about blood. They say it is old-fashioned; they call it "a slaughter-house religion." "For the life of the flesh is in the blood: and I have given it [the blood] to you upon the altar to make an atonement for your souls: for it is the blood that maketh an atonement for the soul" (Lev. 17:11).

This is God's plan, and we must accept it. We are not saved by imitating Christ's example or by admiring His teaching. We are not saved by His character. We are saved by His shed blood. There was an appointed price to pay.

An Appointed Procedure

Sixth, there was *an appointed procedure.* The first thing the priest had to do was to kill the bullock for a sin offering for himself (Lev. 16:11). Then he took the incense into the Holy of Holies. This burning cloud of incense speaks of the glory of God. Salvation is for the glory of God, not just for the good of man (Eph. 1:6,12,14). Then the high priest returned to the altar for the blood; he took it into the Holy of Holies and sprinkled it on the mercy seat, which was the ark of the covenant. The two tables of the Law were in the ark, and Israel had broken that Law. But the blood covered the broken Law. It was the blood that made atonement.

Then the high priest came back to the altar where two goats were waiting. He would kill one goat and take the blood into the Holy of Holies. That blood he sprinkled on the mercy seat. He then applied some of that blood to the brazen altar (Lev. 16:18). Then he returned to the second goat and did an interesting thing. The priest put his hands on the head of the living goat and confessed the sins of the people of Israel. Then that goat was taken out and turned loose in the wilderness, never to be seen again. "As far as the east is from the west, so far hath he removed our transgressions from us" (Ps. 103:12). These two goats together were called a sin-offering. One died; the other (called the scapegoat) was turned loose. Jesus Christ died, He arose again, He went back to heaven. John the Baptist said, "Behold the Lamb of God, which taketh away the sin of the world" (John 1:29). Christ's sacrifice does not just cover sin—He takes our sins away. The release of the scapegoat pictured the truth that the sins of the people had been taken away.

The high priest would then wash and clothe himself again in his garments, a picture of the fact that when our Lord finished His sacrificial work, He returned to heaven and took His throne of glory.

An Appointed Response

Finally, there was *an appointed response on the part of the people*. What was this response? "Ye shall afflict your souls. . . . And ye shall do no work in that same day" (Lev. 23:27,28). Salvation is not by *our* works. The people did nothing. The priest did it all. They were not allowed to work. Instead, they were to show sorrow for their sin and, by faith, to accept what God had provided for them. The annual Day of Atonement speaks to us of God's love and God's grace. There is nothing we can do. "Not by works of righteousness which we have done, but according to his mercy he saved us" (Titus 3:5).

Be God's guest! He will take away your sins!

Chapter 9

Day of Atonement: God's Sinful People

On the tenth day of the seventh month, the activity of the nation of Israel came to a standstill. The high priest was permitted to enter into the Holy of Holies and offer the blood of the sacrifice on the Day of Atonement. We have studied this event and discovered the seven different appointments on the Day of Atonement. But there is much more for us to learn. There are three pictures to be seen in the Day of Atonement: the work of Jesus Christ, the future cleansing of Israel and the future cleansing of the Church.

Let me make it very clear that the basic interpretation of this passage (Lev. 16) relates to the nation of Israel, but there is a spiritual application for us as believers. All Scripture is profitable for us. We don't want to "spiritualize" this chapter and make applications that are not there! But neither do we want to miss the lessons that God has for us.

The Work of Jesus Christ

The annual Day of Atonement illustrates the work of our Lord Jesus Christ. All of the work done on the Day of Atonement was accomplished by one person—the high priest. Aaron, the high priest, was chosen to do this special work (Lev. 16:2). "There shall be no man in the tabernacle of the congregation when he goeth in to make an atonement in the holy place" (v. 17). He had to do it alone.

The only Person who can do this work of salvation for us is Jesus Christ. Just as the high priest laid aside his garments and put on the simple linen garments of a servant, so our Lord Jesus laid aside His garments of glory, came to this earth, became a servant and died for us. The difference, of course, is this: The high priest had to offer sacrifices for himself, but Jesus needed no sacrifice. He was the holy and spotless Lamb of God.

Something else is true: The high priest offered the sacrifice of animals, but the Lord Jesus Christ offered *Himself* as a sacrifice. He did not offer the blood of bulls and goats because the blood of bulls and goats cannot take away sin (Heb. 10:4).

The work of the high priest on the Day of Atonement was the work of atonement. One meaning of the word "atonement" is *to cover*. The blood covered the sins—it could not take the sins away. When Jesus died, He took away the sins of the world. He finished the work once and for all.

When the priest was presented to do his work on the Day of Atonement, he was washed, a picture of sanctification. (Sanctification simply means being set apart.) Our Lord Jesus Christ sanctified Himself to die for us. He said, "For their sakes I sanctify myself" (John 17:19). Our Lord Jesus set Himself apart to do the one task that nobody else could do;

namely, the task of completing salvation for a sinful world. He alone could do it. He alone would do it. He alone is our Saviour today.

The important part of this Day of Atonement ceremony involved the two goats, which, together, were a sin offering (Lev. 16:5): "And he shall take of the congregation of the children of Israel two kids of the goats for a sin-offering." The first goat was slain and the blood applied. "Then shall he kill the goat of the sin-offering, that is for the people, and bring his blood within the vail, and do with that blood as he did with the blood of the bullock, and sprinkle it upon the mercy seat, and before the mercy seat: and he shall make an atonement for the holy place, because of the uncleanness of the children of Israel, and because of their transgressions in all their sins" (vv. 15,16). Jesus died as a sin offering. In fact, when He died on the cross, He was *made sin*. He knew no sin, and He committed no sin; and yet, He died as a sin offering.

What about the second goat? "And when he hath made an end of reconciling [atoning for] the holy place, and the tabernacle of the congregation, and the altar, he shall bring the live goat: and Aaron shall lay both his hands upon the head of the live goat, and confess over him all the iniquities of the children of Israel, and all their transgressions in all their sins, putting them upon the head of the goat, and shall send him away by the hand of a fit man into the wilderness: and the goat shall bear upon him all their iniquities unto a land not inhabited: and he shall let go the goat in the wilderness" (vv. 20-22).

The first goat was slain; the second goat (alive) was turned loose. It is a picture of John 1:29: "Behold the Lamb of God, which taketh away the sin of the world." It also illustrates Psalm 103:12: "As far as the east is from the west, so far hath he removed our transgressions from us."

These two goats picture to us the two aspects of our Lord's work on the cross: He died for us and He arose again. His blood takes away sin. The work that He did never has to be done again. The Old Testament record tells us that the Day of Atonement had to be repeated annually. Every year the same sacrifices, every year the same ceremony. The priest in the Old Testament had an unfinished work. But the Lord Jesus Christ has finished His work. He has put on His robes of glory, and He has gone back to heaven. "But this man, after he had offered one sacrifice for sins for ever, sat down on the right hand of God" (Heb. 10:12).

The Future Cleansing of Israel

Second, this ceremony is a beautiful picture of the future cleansing of Israel. We learned in our study of the Feast of Trumpets that one day God will call His elect people Israel back to the land of Palestine. In Matthew 24:29-31, we read about the trumpet's being blown and the angels of God gathering God's people Israel back to the land. The same truth is stated in Isaiah 27:12,13.

"In that day there shall be a fountain opened to the house of David and to the inhabitants of Jerusalem for sin and for uncleanness" (Zech. 13:1). In what

84

day? In that future day when Jesus Christ shall return. "And it shall come to pass in that day, that I will seek to destroy all the nations that come against Jerusalem. And I will pour upon the house of David, and upon the inhabitants of Jerusalem, the spirit of grace and of supplications: and they shall look upon me whom they have pierced, and they shall mourn for him, as one mourneth for his only son, and shall be in bitterness for him, as one that is in bitterness for his firstborn" (12:9,10).

When the Lord Jesus Christ shall return, Israel shall look upon Him whom they have pierced, and they shall mourn because of their sin. As a result of this, there shall be a time of cleansing and purification, and the fountain shall be opened for sin and for uncleanness (13:1).

We who are New Testament Christians know what that fountain is:

> There is a fountain filled with blood
> Drawn from Immanuel's veins,
> And sinners plunged beneath that flood
> Lose all their guilty stains.

"For I would not, brethren, that ye should be ignorant of this mystery, lest ye should be wise in your own conceits; that blindness in part is happened to Israel, until the fulness of the Gentiles be come in. And so all Israel shall be saved: as it is written, There shall come out of Sion the Deliverer, and shall turn away ungodliness from Jacob: for this is my covenant unto them, when I shall take away their sins" (Rom. 11:25-27). There shall be a future gathering and a future cleansing of the nation of

85

Israel. That is the basic interpretation of the Day of Atonement.

The Future Cleansing of the Church

However, there is an application to the Church. You see, the Church is not all that she ought to be. "Husbands, love your wives, even as Christ also loved the church, and gave himself for it; that he might sanctify and cleanse it with the washing of water by the word, that he might present it to himself a glorious church, not having spot, or wrinkle, or any such thing; but that it should be holy and without blemish" (Eph. 5:25-27).

We must be honest and admit that we, as individual Christians and as the Church collectively, are far from glorious and far from being free of spots, wrinkles and blemishes. But one of these days, the Church will be a glorious Church without spot and wrinkle and without blemish when we stand before the Lord.

Spots come from defilement on the outside. Wrinkles come from decay on the inside. Blemishes come from disease on the inside. Today the Bride of Jesus Christ, the Church, is not as glorious as she ought to be, but one day she shall be glorious. When will this take place? It will take place after the Judgment Seat of Christ.

The Feast of Trumpets, on the first day of the seventh month, pictures the gathering together of God's people. The basic interpretation is for Israel, but there is an application to the Church. The trumpet is going to sound, and we shall be called up to be with the Lord. Then we shall have our heavenly "Day of Atonement." We shall stand before the Lord and give an accounting of our lives and ministries. The Church will have all the wrinkles taken out and all the spots removed and all the blemishes taken care of. Then it will be a glorious Church to the glory of God.

However, we should start that cleansing today. We need "the washing of water by the word" (Eph. 5:26). "Now ye are clean through the word which I have spoken unto you," said the Lord Jesus (John 15:3). Let's keep our lives clean. Let's keep the Church as clean as we possibly can to the glory of God.

Be God's guest and share in "the beauty of holiness" (II Chron. 20:21).

Chapter 10

Tabernacles: God's Suffering People

The Feast of Tabernacles was the last of the seven events listed on God's calendar. "Also in the fifteenth day of the seventh month, when ye have gathered in the fruit of the land, ye shall keep a feast unto the Lord seven days: on the first day shall be a sabbath, and on the eighth day shall be a sabbath. And ye shall take you on the first day the boughs of goodly trees, branches of palm trees, and the boughs of thick trees, and willows of the brook; and ye shall rejoice before the Lord your God seven days. And ye shall keep it a feast unto the Lord seven days in the year. It shall be a statute for ever in your generations: ye shall celebrate it in the seventh month. Ye shall dwell in booths seven days; all that are Israelites born shall dwell in booths: that your generations may know that I made the children of Israel to dwell in booths, when I brought them out of the land of Egypt: I am the Lord your God" (Lev. 23:39-43).

The Feast of Tabernacles is the equivalent of the American or the Canadian "Thanksgiving Day" when the harvest is brought in and the people rejoice at the goodness of the Lord. For seven days the Jewish people lived in booths, reminding them of their pilgrim journey when they were delivered from Egypt.

God Wants His People to Have Joy

There are some very practical lessons from this particular feast, and the first of them is rather obvious: *God wants His people to have joy.* Some people don't believe that. They think that God is somewhat of a "celestial spoilsport," that He sits in heaven trying to figure out ways to make people miserable. Of course, that simply isn't true. God wants His people to have joy. To begin with, He wants us to be able to look back and have joy. God wanted to remind the people that He had led them out of Egypt and had led them through the wilderness. He had been good to them.

It is a good thing to sit down, look back and remember the goodness of the Lord. Over and over again in the Book of Deuteronomy the people were told to remember. Moses said, "Now you remember, you were servants, slaves, in bondage in the land of Egypt, and God delivered you with a mighty hand and with great power." Over and over again Moses said, "Now, when you move into the land of Canaan, when you live in houses you didn't build, when you drink from wells you didn't dig, when you eat from fields and trees that you didn't plant or cultivate, remember this: It's God who has given this to you" (see Deut. 5:15; 6:10-12; 15:15; 16:12; 24:18,22).

As a pastor I have married many young couples. It is interesting to watch them. When they get started in housekeeping, they are grateful for anything they get. But then as they start getting along, they make a little more money and get a promotion, then something happens—they forget. They forget their original beginning. They forget that they had to get started the hard way. Now, I realize some couples get started in pretty good shape. But by and large, most of us got our start the hard way—we had to crawl before we could walk, we had to walk before we could run. It is easy to forget God's past mercies.

The Feast of Tabernacles was a reminder to the Jewish people that everything they had came from God. We need to remember this as a nation. We need to remember this as churches. Sometimes the younger generation in a church takes everything for granted—the church building, the ministry. But you should remember that people sacrificed, worked and gave that the building and ministry might be there. Don't take the ministry of your church for granted. Somebody paid a price. Look back and be grateful for God's past mercies.

But God also wants us to be grateful for the present blessings. Tabernacles was a harvest festival (v. 39). "Thou shalt observe the feast of tabernacles seven days, after that thou hast gathered in thy corn and thy wine: and thou shalt rejoice in thy feast, thou, and thy son, and thy daughter, and thy manservant, and thy maidservant, and the Levite, the stranger, and the fatherless, and the widow, that are within thy gates. Seven days shalt thou keep a solemn feast unto the Lord thy God in the place which the Lord shall choose: because the Lord thy God shall bless thee in all thine increase, and in all the works of thine hands, therefore thou shalt surely rejoice" (Deut 16:13-15).

Jewish tradition added two practices to the Feast of Tabernacles not recorded in Leviticus. For one thing, they used to go down to the Pool of Siloam in Jerusalem, draw out some water and pour it out as a reminder that God gave them water in the wilderness. Jesus made use of this practice when He said, "If any man thirst, let him come unto me, and drink" (John 7:37).

Also, they had four huge candlesticks in the temple court, and every night during that week, these were lighted. It was a reminder of the pillar of fire that guided Israel in the wilderness. Jesus also made use of this when He said in John 8:12, "I am the light of the world."

So the Jewish people could look back and be thankful for God's provision, protection and direction. They once lived in booths—now they were living in houses. They once had to wander—now they were settled down. They once had to ask Him for water—now they had plenty of water. They could rejoice over past and present mercies from the generous hand of God. "Charge them that are rich in this world, that they . . . trust [not] in uncertain riches, but in the living God, who giveth us richly all things to enjoy" (I Tim. 6:17). Enjoy what God has given to you, and employ it for His glory and for the good of others.

Joy Always Follows Cleansing

There is a second lesson: *Joy always follows cleansing*. First the Day of Atonement, then the Feast of Tabernacles.

Nothing will rob you of joy like sin. David said, "Restore unto me the joy of thy salvation" (Ps. 51:12). Sin robs us of joy, but joy always follows cleansing. This was true of the Prodigal Son. When he was out in the world, living with the pigs, rebelling against his father, he was miserable. Then he said, "I'm going home!" He went home, and the father received him and forgave him, and there was great joy. First the cleansing and then the joy. First sin has to be taken care of, and then there can be happiness. God wants His people to have joy, and joy follows cleansing.

Joy Leads to Sacrifice

There's a third lesson we should learn: *Joy leads to sacrifice*. During the Feast of Tabernacles, 199 different animals were sacrificed. Numbers 29 gives you the details on this: Seventy bullocks would be sacrificed and 14 rams and 98 lambs and seven goats. And then on the eighth day there would be one bullock and one ram and one goat and seven lambs. This is a total of 199 animals.

When you are joyfully thankful to God, sacrifice is no problem. God says to us, "I have been good to you. Now you must share. Share with Me. Share with the fatherless and with the widows." Some of you are probably in churches that are having building programs or special missionary programs, and there is a need for money. The economy being what it is, sometimes money is rather hard to come by. Remember that *joy always leads to sacrifice.* When we are happy in the Lord, rejoicing in His goodness, it is no problem at all to share what God gives us. Jesus Christ became poor that we might be rich (see II Cor. 8:9).

I used to ask myself the question, "Why did God stop with 199 animals? Why not an even 200 sacrifices?" And then it came to me—*I* am supposed to be sacrifice number 200. "I beseech you therefore, brethren, by the mercies of God, that ye present your bodies a living sacrifice, holy, acceptable unto God, which is your reasonable service" (Rom. 12:1). When our all is given to Him, it is no problem to sacrifice for others.

The Greatest Joy Is Yet to Come

There is a fourth lesson—*the greatest joy is yet to come.* I have pointed out that the seven feasts of the Lord present God's prophetic program. God's calendar begins with Passover—the death of Christ. Then the Feast of Unleavened Bread—the cleansing of our lives. The Feast of Firstfruits pictures the resurrection of the Lord. Pentecost speaks of the coming of the Holy Spirit. Now, what lies in the future? The Feast of Trumpets—the gathering together of God's people (God's earthly people, Israel, and God's heavenly people, the Church). Then the Day of Atonement when Israel shall be cleansed of her sin and look upon Him whom she pierced. Then shall come that glorious Feast of

93

Tabernacles when Israel shall enter into her kingdom.

We believe that there is a future for Israel. We believe the Bible teaches that one day Jesus Christ shall reign and there shall be a kingdom here on earth. "And his feet shall stand in that day upon the mount of Olives, which is before Jerusalem on the east. . . . And the Lord shall be king over all the earth: in that day shall there be one Lord, and his name one. . . . And it shall come to pass, that every one that is left of all the nations which came against Jerusalem shall even go up from year to year to worship the King, the Lord of hosts, and to keep the feast of tabernacles" (Zech. 14:4,9,16). The Feast of Tabernacles is a picture of that future kingdom when "Jesus shall reign where'er the sun / Does his successive journeys run."

The Feast of Tabernacles will be a time of great rejoicing. God will deliver all nature from the bondage of sin.

The greatest joy is yet to come. There shall be a time when nature will be delivered from the bondage of sin, when you and I will enter into the glory of the Lord, when His Kingdom is established.

Don't fix your heart on the joys of this world because they will not last. And don't get discouraged because you are going through some difficulty— it will not last either. "Weeping may endure for a night, but joy cometh in the morning" (Ps. 30:5). The best is yet to come! Our Lord Jesus is going to come. One day He shall establish His Kingdom, and we shall reign with Him.

94

God wants His people to have joy. Joy always follows cleansing. Joy leads to sacrifice. And the greatest joy is yet to come. Have you trusted Christ as your Saviour? Have you entered into the joy of the Lord?

Be God's guest! The best is yet to come!

Perhaps you cannot accept God's invitation to be His guest because you have never trusted His Son, Jesus Christ, as your Saviour. God has provided salvation as a free gift; you need only receive it. To do so, you must believe that Christ died for *your* sins, was buried and rose again (II Cor. 15:3,4). Place your faith and trust in Him as your personal Saviour. God's Word promises that He will forgive your sins and give you eternal life (Rom. 6:23). Then thank Him for making you His child (John 1:12).

If you have trusted Christ as a result of reading this book, please write and tell us about your decision. We'll be happy to answer any questions you may have, and we'll send you some helpful literature.

Back to the Bible Broadcast
Box 82808, Lincoln, Nebraska 68501